Candid Conversations

Candid Conversations

Real Women. Real Life. Real Faith.

Heather Hart
& Contributing Authors

Candid Conversations
Real Women. Real Life. Real Faith.

Table of Contents

Let's Be Honest

Heather Hart

What is one thing you struggle with as a Christian woman? I asked that question on Facebook one day and the responses started pouring in. One of the first women to comment answered with a question of her own, "Just one?"

In fact, most of the women who responded listed multiple struggles in their answers. They ranged from common to tragic. Many women struggled with patience and pride. Some women struggled making friends while others struggled with submission. Some women were struggling with contentment, and others were struggling with commitment. But not a single woman responded saying she didn't struggle with anything.

We all struggle with something. Life. Faith. Family. Work. Love. Learning. PMS. Menopause. It seems like just when we think we have a handle on things, another struggle pops up or an old one resurfaces.

Can I be honest with you? I used to look around at other Christian women in awe, thinking everyone other than me had it all together. That these other women had mastered house cleaning, child-rearing, and life. I thought every woman at my church (besides myself) was a solid Proverbs 31 woman and that at any moment I would be found out. That they would realize what an utter failure I was. The problem with that sort of thinking is that it's wrong and it's shallow.

What I have discovered though, is when we take the time to really get to know other women, we realize that all of us have our own share of struggles. Maybe it was immaturity or inexperience on my part not to have realized it sooner, or maybe it's just the way we portray ourselves to those around us. Because whether it is an instinct or a learned behavior, we women tend to fight our hardest to put our best foot forward. We want others to think we have it all together. At the end of the day, we want others to look at us and think, "Wow, that lady has a ton on her plate, but she gets it done and she looks good doing it." We wear our "Hot Mess"[1] badges with pride, don't we ladies?

I am definitely a mess. I have no doubt about that, and I am thankful for clichés like "God can turn our mess into His message," and "Our mess is His masterpiece." Sayings such as these don't just tell me I am not alone in this, they remind me that God's got this. He is in control.

I will never forget the first time I heard another Christian woman confess her struggle with depression. This woman, who I idolized, was a pastor's daughter. She was super fit and an amazing mom. She had gorgeous hair and trendy clothes. But as she sat there in our Bible study group pouring her heart out, I was stunned. I thought if this amazing lady had issues, maybe I was okay. Maybe it was okay that I had struggles,

---

[1] Dictionary.com defines a Hot Mess as "a person or thing that is a mess, as in being disorganized, confused, or untidy, yet remains attractive or appealing"

too. Maybe they wouldn't snub me if they knew how much I was struggling with life as a stay-at-home mom, or just how many cheerios were under my couch.

I would love to tell you that my struggle with my struggles ended there, but it didn't. While I learned I could trust that group of women, I thought maybe they were unique. That other women really did have it together, and we were just birds of a feather. I loved their honesty and, for the first time in my adult Christian life, I felt like I belonged.

These women became my closest friends. They were my church family in a way I had never experienced before. Eventually, life happened, and my family and I ended up in a new church. I was in a different Bible study group with new women. These women surely didn't struggle. The mom's home that we met in was always spotless. The women took turns bringing snacks and everyone took the time to study the lesson in advance. These women were most definitely Proverbs 31 women.

One day I just couldn't take it anymore. I arrived a bit early and I asked the hostess how she kept her house so clean with children at home, and her answer rocked me to the core. Are you ready for it? She simply said she didn't. She told me the reason she volunteered to host the study once a week was so she would put the effort in to clean. She confessed that if I would come any other day of the week, or even just a few hours early, that her home wouldn't be so tidy. Housework was something she struggled with.

Now, I tend to be a bit pessimistic. Not towards other people, but towards myself. My first thought is always, well you may think you struggle, but you don't struggle as much as I do. Have you ever felt that way?

I used to take part in this blog hop where we would all

post pictures of our messy homes. I think the lady started it to show others it was okay if your home wasn't perfect, but even her messes looked tidy to me. Sure, there was an overflowing laundry basked tipped over and spilling onto the carpet, but it was freshly-vacuumed carpet. I couldn't find a place in my home that was clean enough to compare to her mess.

Fast-forward a few years and I found myself doing the exact same thing. I took a picture of what my messy quiet time looked like. You know how all you ever see on Instagram are perfectly poised Bibles and pens? Well, my quiet times don't look like that. I have my Bible and a notebook. Probably a dozen pens and highlighters depending on the day. And all of the above is usually all strung out over a table that needs to be cleaned. My Bible shares the space with paperwork that needs to be done, my half-eaten breakfast, and most likely a few of the kids' toys or school papers that have been abandoned.

My goal in taking my messy quiet time picture was to show that it was okay if your quiet time wasn't neat and tidy, but I carefully positioned the camera so you couldn't tell the floor hadn't been swept... or even picked up. So, after I posted my candid photo, I had to force myself to go back and post it again. The whole unfiltered mess that it was.

Some women believe that sharing our mess should be taboo. That we should set a righteous example for others, not flaunt our failures. They say if we struggle with something, we should keep it quiet and work through it. If needed, we should seek out women who do have it all together and learn from them. Yet if there is anything I have learned in my life, it is that none of us have it all together. Romans 3:10 says, *"As it is written: 'There is no one righteous, not even one.'"*

Can I just say that if you are searching for a Christian woman that has it all together, you are either looking for someone who doesn't exist or a liar. That is why we need Jesus. Jesus came to save us because He knew we could never make it on our own. He didn't come to give us a leg up—a boost in the right direction—so we could take it from there.

He came to save us from our sins. Those sins include the sin of pride and thinking we have risen above our sinful nature.

> *"For God so loved the world, that he gave his only Son, that whoever believes in him should not perish but have eternal life."*
> ~ John 3:16

We are all sinners in need of a Savior, thankfully if you are reading this book, you most likely have already met Him. His name is Jesus. He is the eternal God, conceived of the Spirit, and born of a virgin. God became man to live a perfect life and die a sinner's death. Not because of anything He had done, but to bridge the gap between God and us. He paid the price for our sins. For mine and for yours. And by His wounds we are healed (Isaiah 53:5).

Pretending we are sinless at this point is to deny our need for Jesus. It's saying, "Yeah... I needed Jesus once, but I am good now." And that, sweet friend, is a lie from the pit of Hell (1 John 1:8-10). We need Jesus every single day. Every moment. Because we can't live a perfect life on our own. When we accept Jesus, it's not a once and done event. It's a transformation. It's dying to ourselves and starting a new life where Jesus is our Lord. A life where we still struggle, but Jesus has us covered when we fail.

And fail we will. If that weren't so, James wouldn't have

called us to confess our sins to one another (James 5:16). That's why I believe in being honest about our struggles. It's not about our failures, it's about our need for Jesus.

I call this candid Christianity or being candidly Christian. I want to be candid about my faith. In order to do that, I have to be candid about my life, and that includes my struggles. It includes my need for Jesus. What many of us fail to realize is that when we are honest about our struggles, we can get encouragement and support from other Christian women, and we can also encourage and support others who are going through the same struggles we are. We can bear one another's burdens (Galatians 6:2).

Yet, we get afraid. We focus on our fear of being judged for our sin, and then we fail to obey God's command to confess our sins to one another. Proverbs 28:13 says, *"Whoever conceals their sins does not prosper, but the one who confesses and renounces them finds mercy."* That's why it is important to be candid about our struggles.

Life is hard, being a Christian doesn't change that. Jesus isn't some genie in a bottle waiting to whisk all our cares away, but instead, He is our ever-present help in trouble (Psalm 46:1). Jesus promised us that in this world we would have trouble (John 16:33); pretending otherwise doesn't help anyone. Instead, we should be honest and come together to love and support one another through the struggles of life.

That's why I put this book together. It wasn't so we could focus on our struggles, but to help us see that no matter what we are going through, we don't walk alone. Throughout the pages of this book you will find real-life stories from real Christian women. When I asked women about their struggles, I didn't just ask for one-word answers, I also asked them to share their stories. Because our stories as Christian women aren't really our stories at all, they belong to Jesus. Every story in this book is a testimony to God's goodness. Not to how well a woman coped with what was going on, but how Jesus saw them through.

Before we dig in, let me tell you what these candid conversations aren't. Candid conversations aren't about saying our sins and struggles are no big deal. A struggle, by definition, is an effort. It is about not being okay with our sinfulness or situation. If we ever cease struggling, that is when we should be worried. To stop struggling is to stop growing, to stop improving. It would mean we have stopped reaching for righteousness, that we have decided we are enough. To stop struggling would mean we no longer see our need for Jesus.

In this book, you will read stories of women who are chasing hard after Jesus with all that is in them. Not women who have given up and are content to live in sin, but women who long to be holy. These stories are written by women who want to live like Jesus.

Until the day when we meet Jesus face-to-face, we will all struggle. We will put one foot in front of the other and cling to the cross of Christ. Because it is only through the cross that we have any hope of standing in front of Jesus and hearing the words, *"Well done, good and faithful servant"* (Matthew 25:21).

So, as you read through the stories in this book, I encourage you to start your own conversations on its pages. Don't just read this book and judge the women you are reading about—join the conversation. Make notes in the margins that say, "me too," or "I've been there." Respond to something the author said with a verse from Scripture it made you think of or another thought it stirred.

At the end of each story in this book, you will also have your own opportunity to get candid. I've provided some questions and Scriptures you can use for personal reflections or group discussions. However you use this book, I beg you to remember that it was written by real Christian women and no matter what you are struggling with right now, you are not alone.

> *"If I must boast, I will boast*
> *of the things that show my weakness."*
> ~ 2 Corinthians 11:30

Judgements & Jesus

Heather Hart

Have you ever had someone say something to you that stuck with you for life? I have. Years ago, I was in a group of women from my church doing a study on women counseling women. It was being led by our pastor's wife and she said, "If you tell me you don't judge other people, I am going to judge you." I loved the honesty in that statement and it has stuck with me ever since. Maybe in part because I was one of the ones sitting there thinking I didn't struggle with being judgmental.

Romans 3:23 says, *"for all have sinned and fall short of the glory of God,"* and I think we could apply that to being judgmental as well. The problem is that we are all judgmental. We may judge righteously or unjustly, but we all do it. Every opinion we form is a judgment we pass. Whether it's against ourselves or others.

I already shared about how I struggled with thinking my mess was messier than other women's. That's a judgment. I judge them better than me. I judge myself lacking. I look around and I see women who have perfect hair and gorgeous smiles, and I judge them successful, beautiful, and worthy. But not all my judgments are positive, nobody's are.

We do have control over our judgments though. We can choose to see the best in people, or we can choose to assume the worst. Most of the time I try to see the best. Unless I am in a school zone... (if we are ever in a school zone together, I apologize in advance.) They drive me to repentance regularly. Any other time I assume the car that cut me off is in a hurry or having a bad day, but in a school zone? I just assume they are selfish and inconsiderate. It's all about judgments, and I am most certainly a work in progress, and school zones are just one of my struggles.

The point here isn't to tell you how big of a sinner I am, but to illustrate that we all need Jesus. Me. You. My pastor. Your pastor. My husband. Your husband. My neighbor. Your neighbor. The supermarket clerks. The guy on his cell phone. The mom (or dad) in the school zone. All of us.

And we all need Jesus just the same. The guy at church who yelled at my kids doesn't need Jesus more than I do. The woman in the short skirt, 5-inch heels, and way too much cleavage doesn't need Jesus more than my friend's sweet baby girl. Jesus came for everyone. The angel announcing His birth proclaimed, *"Fear not, for behold, I bring you good news of great joy that will be for all the people"* (Luke 2:10). He didn't add, "especially the prostitutes." He didn't say, "The Pharisees in particular." He didn't look at Martha and tell her to listen up. He brought good news of great joy for everyone.

Keeping that in mind, I try to live by the golden rule. You know, *"Do to others what you would have them do to you"* (Matthew 7:12). I try to apply that to my thinking as well. But it doesn't always work... especially when other Christians are involved.

So here is my confession: I am head over heels in love with Jesus, but I don't always find it easy to love other Christians. I especially find it hard to love women who are lacking in love and humility. Not just the women, but any Christians who fail to love like Christ. That is one of my struggles. Jesus called me to renounce it, and I am working my way through it, but we can probably agree that it is just plain hard to love the unloving.

And just as sure as I am that we need to be willing to admit our failures, I am also sure that not everyone will agree or understand. There will be authors, bloggers, and women who look down on us—who will judge us as unworthy. We will encounter women who want to quiet us or fix us. I have run into a few of the fixing type, and it hurts. It hurts to confess your struggle, brokenness, or sin to someone and have them respond with something other than Jesus.

Another one of those quotes that sticks with me is something Beth Moore said at the Propel Conference in 2016. Unlike the pastor's wife's comment, I don't remember it word-for-word, but I have retained the important part. She said when people ask her how she can handle it (whatever it is) her answer is always Jesus. "How can you handle criticism? Jesus. How can you stand in front of 10,000 women and speak from your heart? Jesus. How can you be you? Jesus."

Again, that's not a direct quote, but you get the picture. It stuck with me because I want Jesus to be my answer for everything. I want someone to look at me and ask, "How can you stay so calm in school zones?" And I want to be able to say, "Jesus." That is the prayer of my heart. It's not just about school zones, it's about life.

I want to be able to live boldly for Jesus to the point where people notice. I want to be able to boldly proclaim our need for Jesus because of Jesus. I want to be able to do it even when it's hard. Even when knowing that getting hurt isn't just a possibility but a reality, I still want to choose to obey because of Jesus.

But I know going in that not everyone's answer is Jesus. I know there will be haters, and God will use those people to stretch me, to teach me to love; and I will probably stumble so I apologize in advance if that's you. I am leaning hard on Jesus as I compile this book, knowing that not only will not everyone appreciate its message and that their words will hurt, but that I might ultimately fail at displaying the love of Christ when my humanity gets in the way.

So, I ask going in that you pray for the women who have bravely shared their stories within these pages and for me as I am praying for you. I pray that the gospel would seep into your heart and that Jesus would shine out. Most of all, I pray that through our struggles you will find hope. Not because we are failures or have had hard lives, but because no matter what you are going through, Jesus is there. Jesus came into the world not to condemn the world but to save it (John 3:17).

With that in mind, I ask that you don't read this book and condemn the women who were willing to open up their hearts and share their stories with you, but read it knowing that God is good. Knowing that in this world we will have struggles, we will fail, but we can take heart because Jesus has overcome the world and He has not abandoned us.

> *"If we have died with him, we will also live with him;*
> *if we endure, we will also reign with him; if we deny*
> *him, he also will deny us; if we are faithless, he*
> *remains faithful—for he cannot deny himself."*
> ~ 2 Timothy 2:11-13

Candid Conversation Starters

1) How do you find yourself judging other people or even yourself?

2) Do you see struggles as a sign of weakness, or as reminders that we all need Jesus?

3) Read John 16:33; Galatians 6:2; Proverbs 28:13; and James 5:16. Do you find it hard to share your struggles with other Christian women? Why do you think that is?

4) Is there another way you related to what Heather shared in this chapter? If so, what was it?

Your Life Is God's Story

Maretha Retief

Everyone has a story to tell. A story with the potential to change lives. A story where God can turn our struggles and ugliness into something beautiful. No matter what place we find ourselves in, God writes His story through our lives. Can you see His words written across the pages of your life?

I had my doubts about whether God was even present at my beginning, but now I know better. Do you think God can only write His story through a well-behaved, flawless, socially accepted life? Think again. I am everything but that and God still chose me, in spite of all my physical, emotional, behavioral, and social flaws to write His story of hope through me.

I was born with a disability on my left hand: I only have a pinkie and a thumb. Cruelty and mockery followed early on. Before I understood what had happened to me, I had to deal with the challenges of other children's opinions about me and I had to make a choice: am I defined by my outward appearance and people's opinions or do I believe that there is more to me?

Initially I chose to deal with my challenges by becoming performance driven. I did not feel accepted as a starting point. Being ignorant of Jesus' thoughts toward me, I chose to earn my acceptance through performance. I began to believe that I should work for everything I wanted to have or feel; that nothing would be given to me on a plate, coated in the blessing of acceptance. I began to journey down a path which brought me to a downward spiral where nothing could break me free except the love of Christ.

Tennis became my safe-haven. I started playing at the age of four and exceeded all expectations. I felt safe and accepted as long as I was on a tennis court... a temporary solution.

As time passed, challenges of jealousy and its companions that walk hand in hand with a physical disability came along, but I was adamant I would not stand back for anything—that hard work and determination would get me through anything. And it did for the most part, but not to the extent of being truly fulfilled in my purpose in life and having peace with who I am.

At the age of 17, I was accepted into the main draw at Junior Wimbledon and what I thought was the essence of living my dream, but everything came to a sudden halt. My prayer for God to let His will be done was answered in a way and at a time I never expected. My tennis career came to an end. My hands could not take all the pressure of playing professional sports and I was brought down to my knees facing just myself and the promise God placed on the table that what He had in store for me was greater than any plans I could have for myself (Jeremiah 29:11). They were plans that not even a physical disability could stop.

I had to choose God and His ways above my own. What felt like a disastrous time became one of the most profound turnaround points of my life. I was left with no performance, few friends, and an awakening to the unconditional love and acceptance of Christ. The presence of a physical disability could not halt God's love and acceptance for me. All that was left was for me to receive it.

After facing many inward struggles and making peace with the fact that my plans are not better than God's plans, I became at rest and began to surrender the ideas I had for myself and handed over the pen to God to continue His story through me. A story, that if I look back after a few years now, I could not have written any better. In fact, I would have completely missed the anticipation and highs of the wonderful blessings of marriage, motherhood, and an abundant life at rest had I kept the pen in my own hand.

Your challenges or setbacks in life may not be a physical disability or something visible, maybe you are facing is an internal or invisible struggle. We all face our own struggles and to each of us they come in the size and manner we can handle with the help of Jesus (1 Corinthians 10:13). I found the key lies in the decision that we should not allow those setbacks, struggles, or challenges to define or limit us, but see them as the perfect opportunities for God to write His great words through them. Nothing is beyond God's reach as He can use all things for the good of those who love Him and have been called according to His purpose (Romans 8:28).

It is okay to face difficulties in life, but I invite you to not let them have the last say. Some of us may have had bad beginnings, and all of us have to cross a mountain at some point in our lives, but let those mountains become the new place from which you look back and see the splendid view God had prepared for you all along in spite of the struggles you had to endure.

You are destined to be a beautiful story with an impact that treads deep footsteps for God's Kingdom. May each day present an opportunity for you where God can write His divine words across the pages of your life. Will you let Him?

Candid Conversation Starters

1) Have you ever let something or someone other than Jesus become your safe-haven? If so, what was it?

2) Romans 8:28 says God can use all things for the good of those who love Him. Do you believe that?

3) Looking back at your life, can you remember a specific time when you thought something was bad, but now you can see it was for the best? Read Romans 8:31-39.

4) Is there another way you related to what Maretha shared in this chapter? If so, what was it?

Living for Jesus

Jaime Hampton

The Story of the Golden Retriever

I am tired. Really, really tired. I know I always seem energetic, enthusiastic and eager to please, but keeping up that façade takes everything I have. It is exhausting running from person to person, performing on cue. But the exhilaration I get from a pat on the head for a job well done is what drives me to carry on. The disappointment that comes when I fail to earn the approval of those around me is crushing.

At my best, I am a loyal, self-sacrificing companion. You won't know when I'm at my worst, because on the outside I will look very much the same. But on the inside... that is another story.

I may not be a dog, but this golden retriever's story is my story. My husband and I attended a marriage conference many years ago and took a personality test that assigned you an animal based on your temperament. I was a golden retriever, and it totally fits; I am a card-carrying people pleaser.

You, too, might be a people pleaser if you:

- hate confrontation
- avoid offending others at all costs
- agree with people to "keep the peace"
- feel almost euphoric when someone gives you praise or acknowledgement
- feel devastated when someone disapproves of you, or becomes angry with you
- have a hard time saying "no" to people
- never feel like you are doing enough

I think I became aware of my people-pleasing tendency sometime around college, or at least at that point I gave it a name. But as time went on, it evolved into "people-pleasing 2.0," which took it to a whole new level. Before, I had been enslaved to the wants and needs of people around me, constantly trying to gain their approval. But later, this inner voice emerged. I am not sure where it came from, but it was always accusing me of failure, anticipating the displeasure of others, even when nobody was around to be displeased.

So where did this voice come from? Maybe I had given Satan a foothold by allowing this people-pleasing trait to grow in me, and the voice was the Accuser himself. Maybe I had gotten so used to guessing what other people wanted from me, that I had begun to anticipate, or even fabricate their expectations. But whoever or whatever the voice was, I became a slave to it; it was a heavy burden that I bore daily.

One morning when the voice had been particularly loud,

I decided I was tired of it. I began to wage war on that voice, hoping to take those incorrect thoughts captive and make them obedient to Christ. I started thinking of scripture about God's love for me and speaking it aloud. And then, almost audibly in my mind, I heard another voice. This time it was the voice of The Shepherd: *"Come to me, all you who are weary and burdened, and I will give you rest. Take my yoke upon you and learn from me, for I am gentle and humble in heart, and you will find rest for your souls"* (Matthew 11:28-29, NIV).

It was like everything else just faded into the background as I rested in those beautiful words. I so wanted to trade in slavery to the inner voice for serving a gentle, humble master who loved me. I longed to throw off that heavy burden of people-pleasing and take on the yoke of Jesus, to learn how to live life to the full. And because of Jesus, it was possible! But old habits are hard to break. I still struggle, but I see the victories coming more frequently, and I recover more quickly from the defeats.

"Jesus replied: 'Love the Lord your God with all your heart and with all your soul and with all your mind.' This is the first and greatest commandment. And the second is like it: 'Love your neighbor as yourself.' All the Law and the Prophets hang on these two commandments.'"
~ Matthew 22:37-40 (NIV)

When you are a people pleaser, you are a lot like that golden retriever who found herself a slave to the many voices around her. Trying to make everyone around you happy is not only exhausting, it is impossible. If you were to ask those who know a people pleaser to describe her in one word, chances are it would be something like "nice." But God doesn't call us to be nice, He calls us to love.

> *"Iron sharpens iron, and one man sharpens another."*
> ~ Proverbs 27:17

Loving God first means that He orders our priorities, not everyone around us. That can mean saying "no" to good things to make room for God's best and (here's the kicker) not feeling guilty about it. Loving our neighbor means sacrificing our need to be liked, or fear of confrontation in the name of speaking truth in love to someone who needs to be challenged. The Bible tells us that, as Christians, we need to "sharpen" each other. That may require friction, and even a little bit of pain. You can't sharpen a sword with a marshmallow.

If you are a recovering people pleaser like me, you may be tempted to despise your people-pleasing qualities; you have become so used to them doing damage that you see them as inherently bad. But God created you. When we see sin manifest in our lives, it is often a distortion of something inherently good, a quality that God can use to further His Kingdom, if we would only submit ourselves to His yoke and learn how. We people pleasers genuinely care about people. We also have the ability to be sensitive and diplomatic, something the Apostle Paul used to gain rapport with others with the goal of sharing the gospel:

"To the Jews I became like a Jew, to win the Jews. To those under the law I became like one under the law (though I myself am not under the law), so as to win those under the

law. To those not having the law I became like one not having the law (though I am not free from God's law but am under Christ's law), so as to win those not having the law. To the weak I became weak, to win the weak. I have become all things to all people so that by all possible means I might save some" (1 Corinthians 9:20-22, NIV).

So, let us go back to our golden retriever. What would it look like if, instead of being distracted by the crowds of people beckoning and whistling for her, she kept her eyes fixed on her master? If she did that, what a freedom she would experience from the heavy burden of pleasing everyone else! She would have clear, consistent expectations. He would be the one to direct her steps and order her priorities.

> *"Am I now trying to win the approval of human beings, or of God? Or am I trying to please people? If I were still trying to please people, I would not be a servant of Christ."*
> ~ Galatians 1:10 (NIV)

There may be times that she is given a specific task, which will mean ignoring the attention of a passerby, even if it means forfeiting a good scratch behind the ears. But because her master knows the needs of those around her even better than she does, he will direct her to the tasks and people where she is most needed. Instead of living life exhausted and scattered, never really feeling like she has done enough, she will curl up peacefully at night knowing she has the approval of the only one who matters. He will pat her on the head and say the words that bring ultimate fulfillment to her soul: "Well done, good and faithful servant."

Candid Conversation Starters

1) Have you ever struggled with being a people-pleaser? Can you remember a specific situation where you let your fear of what other people would think take your eyes off Jesus?

2) How should Galatians 1:10 change the way we live?

3) Is there another way you related to what Jaime shared in this chapter? If so, what was it?

The God Who Hears Me

Sheila Qualls

Let me tell you about the day I downed two large sweet teas at McDonald's. Sixty-four ounces. One right after the other. I am not talking hot-southern-afternoon-sipping-tea-under-the-veranda kind of tea drinking. I am talking college-boy-frat-party chugging kind of drinking.

Honestly, I needed to drown my sorrows. We all have our drug of choice. Mine is sweet tea.

Let me back up. About an hour earlier, I had put my daughter on a bus headed to her first high school retreat. As the bus pulled out of the parking lot, I could see her silhouette through the tinted window. Everyone in the girls' section of the bus was paired up. *Everyone except her.* She sat alone.

I wanted to cry. I wanted to chase the bus down the street and snatch her off. And would have if other parents hadn't surrounded me. Instead, I casually said my goodbyes to the other moms in the parking lot, went to my car and cried.

My daughter struggles with social anxiety, and I struggle every time I put her in a new social situation. When I dropped off her and her brother at the church to get on the bus, I saw a look of panic set in her eyes. I tried to calm her fears by telling her she had a great opportunity to make new friends. I reminded her she was going on a church trip, to pray, and to put her trust in God and watch what He could do. But, I crumbled inside as she boarded the bus.

I wish there was no truth to the events that transpired next, but this is the way it happened (and I am not proud of it). The truth is I didn't feel like putting my trust in God. I was angry and hurt because of the circumstances in my life at that time.

I felt sorry for myself. In the two years prior, I had sent my two oldest kids off to college. My husband had a demanding job and traveled a lot. We had relocated to a new town, left our friends… I felt anxious, angry, and isolated. I spent less and less time with God. Prior to all the disruption in my life, I had felt close to God. Slowly, I had drifted away. Now, I was facing a crisis and feeling alone.

As the bus pulled out, my daughter spotted me in the parking lot, pressed her face to the window, gave me a sad little smile, raised her hand and waved goodbye. I was heartbroken. I drove around for a half an hour, absolutely miserable. All I could think about was her sad little face.

I needed comfort.

That is how I ended up alone in a parking lot sitting under a dimly lit streetlight chugging sweet tea like a college boy at a frat party. But, after downing the second one, I thought, "This is crazy. I am a believing woman. I've led Bible studies. I've mentored people. I can handle this."

I decided to turn to the someone I thought could ease my anxiety, at least my anxiety about the trip…

I called my son. He was on the bus. I told him to sit with his sister until I developed a plan.

It wasn't long before I started beating myself up and blaming people. I blamed the youth group leader, the pastor, the bus company (for having a two-to-a-seat setup). I even debated driving to California (from Colorado) to pick her up or arranging to have her fly home in the morning.

I had just given my daughter the "trust in God and pray" talk. Honestly, I felt like that was a great idea for her. Not for me.

No matter how I looked at the situation, I couldn't come up with solution—at least one that was reasonable. Still, I didn't pray. I felt distant from God. I felt like He wasn't there. Like He couldn't hear me.

I hadn't spent quality, meaningful time with Him in quite a while. I felt hollow. It wasn't like I had altogether forgotten about God. I had set aside time to pray from time to time but would spend most of the time distracted; thinking about grocery shopping, cleaning, home schooling, my loneliness, my fears or any other random topic that ran through my mind. I couldn't seem to connect with Him.

I focused on my circumstances.

Prayer should have been my first response not my last resort. I know it is essential in my walk with Christ. But when things got hectic, my prayer life took the hit. I felt farther and farther away from God.

In the weeks leading up to the retreat, my prayer life had been especially dry. I knew I wasn't experiencing the fullness of my relationship with Christ. I prayed but my prayers were mostly quickies: "Lord, don't let me get stuck in traffic." "Keep my kids safe while they are away from me." "Thank You for this food."

I am ashamed to admit it, but my faith was weak. Somewhere in the back of my mind I thought: *Prayer doesn't work for me anymore.* I was too focused on "doing" to numb my loneliness and not enough on being with God.

I wasn't a new Christian. I knew I should have placed my heartache before the Lord. But I let my circumstances rule my heart. A few times I tried to remind myself that prayer isn't about changing my circumstances; it's about changing my heart. But the thought didn't resonate with me.

I badly needed the Lord's power in that situation with my daughter, *and* in my life as a whole. But I had let circumstances rob me of my relationship with God.

The Lord tells us in Psalm 34:18, *"He is close to the brokenhearted and rescues those whose spirits are crushed."* I am so glad I serve a God who never lets go. Who stays close in times of distress and pain.

About two hours after I put my daughter on that bus, I was reduced to shame, another sign of my neglect of my relationship with God. I knew He was there, but my heart was hardened. I was afraid to cry out to Him. I sat in my car, tears streaming down my face. And God spoke to me right where I was. He was there waiting for me.

> *"Refresh my heart in Christ*
> ~ Philemon 1:20b

I dropped my tear-streaked face into my hands. I didn't even know where to begin. I remembered how we had prayed in a Bible study group I had been involved in, so I started to praise Him. I thanked Him. Then I cried out my fears and doubts, and confessed my sin.

That was a tough period in my life. I am thankful I serve a loving, forgiving God who hears me and wants to comfort me even when I veer far from Him.

I didn't hear from my daughter for the rest of the week, yet I was still tempted to worry. But when those fears and doubts crept into my mind, I remembered My First Responder: Jesus Christ. I know I need Him and He is way more refreshing than a gallon of sweet tea.

Candid Conversation Starters

1) What is your go-to stress reliever?

2) Read Psalm 20. Do you trust God to fight for you—to handle tough situations—or do you try to handle everything on your own?

3) Is there another way you related to what Sheila shared in this chapter? If so, what was it?

Finding My Confidence
Phyllis Sather

There I was, at the dreaded office Christmas party... again!

As part of his job, my husband had to attend certain functions, and this was one of them. I didn't belong here with all these doctors, lawyers, and career women. No matter how I said it—housewife, homemaker, or even nest builder—there always seemed to be an "only" in front of it that made the next word seem of little or no consequence.

I was standing inconspicuously in a corner, sipping my punch, hoping Dan would want to leave soon, when I saw Dr. Edwards' wife approaching. My heart sank. She was an attorney. Whatever would I find to say to her? I took a deep breath and tried to remember what Dan had told me. His secret to getting along at these functions was to ask questions, find out what the other person was interested in, and then get them to talk about that.

She introduced herself and I greeted her and said Dan had told me she was an attorney. I asked what type of law she worked in. She replied that she was an attorney for the school district and continued to tell me a little about her job. Then she asked the dreaded question: "What do you do?" I swallowed hard and told her that I was a homemaker and we home educate our three children.

"Why in the world would you want to do that?" she spat at me. I was speechless and just wanted to run and hide. I'm sure I said something, but I don't know what. I knew I was a daughter of the King, and I knew He loved me enough to send His Son to die for my sins, but somehow none of that seemed to matter at that moment.

That wasn't the first or the last time I felt that way: uncomfortable, like I would never fit in. Why did I always feel like I never fit? It seemed like I never measured up to other women. I didn't homeschool as well as others; after all, I didn't even have a college degree. I didn't know how to dress appropriately, which was especially difficult now that I had gained a few pounds. I was even too embarrassed to talk to any of my friends about my feelings. I was sure none of them felt that way.

I finally asked the Lord to show me a better way than just to endure. As I prayed, I was reminded that all I had ever wanted to be was a wife and mother. Other girls dreamed of careers, but not me.

Now I was married to a wonderful man and had three delightful children. Our lives were busy with Dan finishing up his schooling and beginning a new job. We decided to home educate our children and the main portion of that fell to me since Dan was gone much of the time. I found it extremely challenging and rewarding.

I remembered our oldest daughter, Emily, coming to me when she was about six and saying, "Mommy, I know why you homeschool me." When asked why, she replied,

"Because you couldn't bear to be away from me all day." I realized that she was most definitely right. Not only could I not bear it, but I didn't want to be away from her all day.

It might not be everyone's dream job, but it was mine. At that point I realized that I was doing everything I had ever dreamed of doing. Over the next weeks, I studied the Word and put some new thoughts in place in my life that I would like to share with you.

4 Keys To Confident Living

1) Comparison Is The Enemy Of Contentment

If we could take this seriously, we would all be much happier and more content.

Elisabeth Elliot once said, **"It is for us women to receive the given as Mary did, not to insist on the not-given, as Eve did.** Mary received God's call on her life. Eve looked at what she wasn't given, the fruit of the tree of the knowledge of good and evil, and wanted it. When I compare myself to another, in a way I am wondering: *Why wasn't I given that in the way that she was?"* (emphasis added).

2) Take Your Thoughts Captive

2 Corinthians 10:5 says, *"We destroy arguments and every lofty opinion raised against the knowledge of God, and take every thought captive to obey Christ."*

We can prevent many difficulties if we strive to take our thoughts captive. I would encourage you to think about where your thoughts are coming from: the Lord, yourself, or our enemy. Learn to discern who is putting thoughts into your mind and treat them accordingly. **You don't need to believe everything you think.**

3) Pray

Matthew 5:44 says, *"But I say to you, Love your enemies and pray for those who persecute you."*

I know these women aren't my enemies, but our real enemy would like them to be. I am teaching myself to pray when I feel jealous of another woman's gifts. I also try to find a way to compliment her on them.

4) Don't Be Anxious

Philippians 4:5-7 tells us, *"The Lord is at hand; do not be anxious about anything, but in everything by prayer and supplication with thanksgiving let your requests be made known to God. And the peace of God, which surpasses all understanding, will guard your hearts and your minds in Christ Jesus."*

We have probably all memorized the above verse at one time or another, but I suddenly discovered the words just before "do not be anxious"—"The Lord is at hand." Now that is a great reason not to be anxious. As I prepared for the next business event, I found myself praying about the women I would talk with.

As I made a point to share these things with Mrs. Edwards, my enthusiasm grew, and I must have told her considerably more than she really wanted to hear. She finally excused herself to talk with someone else. I breathed a sigh of relief but not because I was glad to have her leave, as I would have been in our prior conversation. I was a new person, more confident in my role as wife, mother, homeschool mom, and homemaker.

I was doing exactly what I always wanted to do. How many people can say that?

Candid Conversation Starters

1) How have you struggled with insecurity? Can you remember a specific time you felt insecure or anxious? When was it?

2) Read Matthew 5:44 and Romans 12:14. Have you ever prayed for a woman who made you feel insecure? If so, what was the result?

3) Is there another way you related to what Phyllis shared in this chapter? If so, what was it?

A Servant's Heart

Jessica Wright

Quiet and confident is not how I would typically describe myself. I would say my Christian walk would be described as clamorous and unsure. You see, if I had to choose whom I better relate to, Martha or Mary, I would have to say Martha. And, frankly, for a long time I didn't like that, but I couldn't help it. That was my modus operandi, my M.O., my method.

When you read the story about Martha and Mary in Luke 10, you see two sisters who are hosting dinner for their special guest, Jesus. One of them is busy in the kitchen fixing dinner and the other is conversing with Jesus. For years I read this scripture with the mindset that this story was placed in the Bible to show us a definite division. Like, you are one or the other, either a Martha or a Mary. One is bad, and the other is good.

Because I saw being a Mary as good, for years I wrestled with being a Martha while trying with everything in my strength to be a Mary. Spiritual gifting tests would tell me that was just who I was, but for some reason that didn't sit well with me. I am not saying there is anything wrong or unspiritual about service as a spiritual gift—quite the contrary. But I knew my serving was not done with the right heart. I would work hard and serve where I knew I could serve, but I did all my serving out of a need to fill a void.

Over the past few years, I believe God has been teaching me what was at the heart of this dinner with Martha and Mary. I now believe it's not about whether I am a Martha or a Mary. We can all have the tendency to think like Martha, but God has called us all to be Mary. And to go a little further, I don't believe Martha was the unspiritual one. I just think she got distracted.

Both Martha and Mary had a relationship with Jesus, and Mary was not the more spiritual one. When their brother Lazarus died, as recorded in John 11, Martha is the one who ran to Jesus and said, *"Lord, if You had been here, my brother would not have died. Even now I know that whatever You ask of God, God will give You."* (vs 21-22, NASB) Martha knew Jesus, she knew His power, she knew His heart. She knew **Him**.

I believe the story of Martha and Mary's dinner with Jesus is not about who is more spiritual or who is better. You see, I believe Martha and Mary both had servant hearts, and they both had a relationship with Jesus. However, on this particular night Martha puts us in the story, and Jesus speaks to her heart and ours as well.

You and I are Marys when we are confidently quiet in the presence of God. Mary is who we are when we know who God is and we know our identity in Him. The Mary mindset assures us that we are His children and His friends. We know that nothing can separate us from His love. We know that we are righteous because of nothing we have done and everything Jesus has done. Jesus' blood has made us right

> *"No longer do I call you servants, for a servant does not know what his master is doing; but I have called you friends, for all things that I heard from My Father I have made known to you."*
> ~ John 15:15 (NASB)

with God. When He looks at us, a righteous child is who He sees. Mary knew she was a friend of Jesus.

Martha is who we are when we forget this.

We act like Martha when we believe the lie that we have to earn His pleasure and approval. Instead of just coming to Jesus and confessing her thoughts and feelings to the one who would show her the truth, Martha started doing. We act like Martha when we lose sight and forget we are Jesus' friend and go back to acting like servants.

Don't we all have that tendency? When our relationship with God seems shaky or distant, instead of just coming to Him and bearing our hearts to Him, we assume. We start "doing" to win His pleasure, favor, and approval.

Bill Johnson says it best in his book *Dreaming with God*: "Most servants want to degrade the role of the friend to feel justified in their works-oriented approach to God. Jesus' response is important to remember: *'Mary has chosen the better part.'* Martha was making sandwiches that Jesus never ordered. Doing more for God is the method servants use to increase in favor…Mary wasn't a non-worker; she just learned to serve from His presence, only making the sandwiches that Jesus ordered."[2]

When we know who we are and know the depth of our

---

[2] Johnson, Bill. *Dreaming with God*. Shippensburg, PA. Destiny Image® Publishers Inc. 2006.

relationship with God, we can be quiet and confident. We can turn our focus to seeking His presence rather than His approval. When we do that, we are freed from religion that tells us, "You need to do more, you're not doing enough, you have to make Him approve of you." We can live in the place where we can say: *"'My heart, O God, is quiet and confident all because of you'* (Psalm 108:1, TPT) I know who You are, God, and I know who I am in You."

Candid Conversation Starters

1) Take a moment to read the story of Martha and Mary (Luke 10:38-42). Who can you relate to more, Martha or Mary? Why?

2) Read Psalm 37:7, 62:5, and 46:10. Do you ever have trouble sitting quietly with Jesus and just being still?

3) Is there another way you related to what Jessica shared in this chapter? If so, what was it?

I Am Not Alone

Cristine Eastin

I am a suicide survivor, a confusing term, I think—it sounds like *I* survived a suicide attempt. But, no, it was my mother; she killed herself.

I have never tried to remember the exact date, or the age she was when she died, but I know it was the first week in April of 1973, when I was twenty-two and she was in her mid-forties. She sat in the car in the garage with the motor running.

I don't remember crying on the drive from Peoria to St. Paul—not until I got to my in-laws' house. My mother-in-law met me on the sidewalk, enveloped me in a huge hug, and said, "In time you'll remember the good times with your mother."

Then I cried. I wish those words had come true. I was angry… More than angry. I was enraged.

At my mother's memorial service, our family sat in the balcony. I looked down at the 500-600 people who crowded the sanctuary and wondered how my mother had touched so many people when she and I didn't seem to like each other

49

much. I shook off someone's comforting hand, put on my denial face, and talked with dear family friends at the reception—stuffing my raging grief way down deep where even I couldn't touch it.

Within three months of my mother's death I moved overseas for three and a half years. I was in a new, not-very-good marriage; I drank too much, and I slept till noon for something to do. I threw myself into theatre, skiing, friends—anything, as long as I was busy. And if anyone asked me how my parents were I said, "Fine."

I was a mess.

Spiritually? I hadn't talked to God for years, and I called myself an agnostic. Whether God existed or not didn't matter to me. My mother's death pushed me further from God. I was a closed tight shell. Let me tell you, when your mother leaves this life, and therefore you, of her own choice—that is an abandoned feeling that goes all the way to the bottom of the well with no bucket in sight.

I'll spare you the gory years, but in 1982 I started dating a Christian man, and I met Christians who I didn't think were nuts. I started seeking God, not to please this guy in my life, but for myself. We laugh now (we have been married thirty-three years) about the time we stood outside the camper van in Yellowstone, looking up at the sky, and I said, "We're not alone." (Right! Mama grizzly and her cub were in our campsite!) Anyway, I was getting to know God, and He was becoming real to me. I believed the scripture, *"Never will I leave you; never will I forsake you"* (Hebrews 13:5, NIV). I felt loved and I committed my life to Jesus.

I had hope, something my mother apparently didn't have enough of. One of the not-crazy Christians gave me this scripture: *"No eye has seen, no ear has heard, no mind has conceived what God has prepared for those who love him"* (1 Corinthians 2:9, NIV). So I accepted that God's love was on a plane so far above and so different from my experience of human love, that the planes never intersected, which was a good thing. I decided that my over-educated, over-busy mind could just give up trying to figure out this faith thing and accept it. Well, that was no doubt the Holy Spirit whispering in my ear, not my human thoughts.

I started training as a psychotherapist, and it was harder to keep a lid on my denial when I was faced with potentially dealing with suicidal clients. I was afraid I might take out my irrational rage on a client and tell them, "Just jump! See if I care!" Oh, yes, I was still angry.

A supervisor for a clinical practicum asked me a simple, but powerful question about a suicidal client who had had an abortion: "What's your goal for her?"

Me: "To keep her alive, of course."

Supervisor: "Can you do that?"

Realization dawned and shone a light down some deep cracks in me. No, I couldn't keep her alive.

I was in therapy at the time with a therapist to whom I am forever grateful. She backed me into a verbal corner where I realized I was about to say that I felt responsible in some way for my mother's suicide. I had been a difficult child, according to my mother, and I must have always believed, way down in that well, that I was responsible in part for her unhappiness—otherwise, why would she have left us?

That is when the healing started. I acknowledged that anger—that grief. But I still kept it on a pretty high shelf.

A few years later, while washing dishes Christmas Eve, I started sobbing for no apparent reason. I realized that Christmas Eve was the last time I had seen my mother alive.

I started to work more actively on my grief. Not everything was helpful, such as hearing: "the preventing of a suicide is not necessarily the saving of a life." How thoughtless to say something like that.

I learned that asking "Why?" isn't productive. There is no answer to that question that will adequately explain what happened and certainly no answer that I can accept. I don't know what my mother was going through; I know a few of her demons, but only she knew her pain and hopelessness.

I wish I could have been mature enough in the Lord and in myself to offer her the scripture *"Now faith is being sure of what we hope for and certain of what we do not see"* (Hebrews 11:1, NIV). At least I have said that to many clients since.

Then, several years ago, my husband and I were at a large Christian gathering. He had gone to the back for prayer leaving me at our seats. I felt a comforting arm around my shoulder—so real and firm a touch that I looked to see who was there. This time I didn't shake it off. But there was no one there. The words, "You have been delivered from the spirit of loneliness," came to mind. I felt loved.

I won't say it's all better; it never will be. But I am less afraid, less angry—not as sad, when I am holding the Lord's hand, gazing at His face—because then I see my mother, not through *my* eyes, but I see her as a reflection in God's tears.

Candid Conversation Starters

1) Have you ever struggled with feelings brought on by a deep grief? Anger, insecurity, guilt, or something else?

2) Read Psalm 121. Do you look to God to find your hope, no matter what you are going through?

3) Is there another way you related to what Cristine shared in this chapter? If so, what was it?

While I Am Waiting

Beth Kelly

I had no idea how bad it was. I mean, I knew it wasn't the best between my husband and me, but I figured it was the normal stressors of life every couple goes through when trying to manage work, home, and young children.

I was **wrong**.

By the time I realized we were on the brink of the end, it was too late. We became separated and now lived 20 minutes from each other. Desperate for a restored marriage, I tried every trick in the book. My efforts were fruitless, and only served to drive a bigger wedge between us.

I was devastated.

I did the only thing left there was to do, and I prayed. It was the kind of prayer that you buckle your knees in anguish, sorrow, and desperate plea: "Lord! Please save my marriage and my family!"

The next six months were heart wrenching. I never knew I could hurt so bad. There were days that just making it through one more minute felt exhausting. However, thanks to a few wise and godly girlfriends of mine who kept encouraging me, I continued to seek God's will for my life and my marriage.

My girlfriends didn't tell me what I wanted to hear. They spoke Gods' truths to me every time I complained. I started seeking God's Word on my own, and over time the Bible came alive to me.

I started learning what it truly meant to be a godly wife. I learned what it really was to give grace to my husband in all things. I experienced the power of God to work on our behalf when we fervently pray, and I experienced His peace when things felt impossible and scary.

My faith in God grew ten-fold over those six months.

Two weeks before Christmas, with God, we beat all worldly odds and moved back in together. We were re-united as a couple and as a family. We didn't have much, but it was the most joyous Christmas, one that I will always cherish.

If you are in the shoes I once was, I encourage you to keep seeking God for direction. He will show you the way.

I would also like to share some Bible verses here that I leaned on many times.

- John 16:33: *"I have said these things to you, that in me you may have peace. In the world you will have tribulation. But take heart; I have overcome the world."*

- Jeremiah 29:11: *"For I know the plans I have for you, declares the Lord, plans for welfare and not for evil, to give you a future and a hope."*

- Psalm 34:18: *"The Lord is close to the brokenhearted; he rescues those whose spirits are crushed."*

Candid Conversation Starters

1) Has God ever used a bad situation to grow your faith? If so, how?

2) When you are going through a hard time, do you cling to Jesus or let the situation rule your heart and mind?

3) How do the verses Beth shared at the end of the chapter help you? Are there any other verse you cling to when the going gets tough?

4) Is there another way you related to what Beth shared in this chapter? If so, what was it?

Uncomfortable Callings
Cheryl Long

I didn't want to write that letter. Sitting there at the table, pen suspended above the lined paper, I tried to think of what to say. ***What does one write to a murderer?***

All wrapped up in my own sheltered life of homeschooling and raising children, I had just given birth to my 7th child and was settling into a routine when I learned of the woman on trial. I don't normally get caught up in drama. In fact, we didn't have television or newspaper, but a neighbor was kind enough to save his papers for fire-starters, as we heated with wood. Crinkling the paper that chilly winter morning, I had noticed the headlines. The story caught my attention because the woman in question was the mom of many children who was on trial for intentionally driving the wrong way on a one-way highway which resulted in the deaths of seven people, including four of her children who were in the car with her that day.

During the days leading up to the trial, our neighbor faithfully delivered the newspaper, though I never asked. I felt compassion for all those affected and figured the woman, who was believed to have been suicidal, would get what she deserved: life in prison.

The first day of the trial a large photo appeared of the woman being led into the courtroom and below the picture were some harsh words quoted by the wife and mother of the victims in the other vehicle: "(she) deserves to burn in hell for what she did." The lady was obviously responding out of deep pain and grief, but I began to consider that if this is the only exposure to Christianity the woman on trial experienced, she was doomed.

As the trial progressed, I began to sense the Lord prompting me to write to the woman. At first I behaved like Moses, with all my excuses. Finally, I relented.

It was not easy writing that first letter, but I did manage to convey "God loves you just as much as He loves anyone else." I went on to tell her about forgiveness through Jesus Christ. I hadn't planned to sign my name but then wondered if she might need a Bible.

Finally, I took the letter to the post office mailbox. As I let go of the envelope this question rang clearly in my mind: *"Are you ready for this?"*

I laughed at my silly melodrama and drove away, believing I had completed my assignment. Several weeks later I found a letter in my mailbox that I never imagined would be there. My hands trembled as I opened the letter and read her words that brought tears to my eyes. "I need a friend like you in my life. Will you continue writing me, please?"

"Are you ready for this?"

I was more than a bit nervous about this whole thing. First of all, I was still somewhat of a babe in Christ (four years saved at the time). What could this woman possibly learn from me?

Then there were the naysayers. As I shared this information with others, I came under condemnation. Some believed that I should not be writing to a convicted killer (she had been found guilty and sentenced to 215 years in prison without parole). Others believed I was not "qualified" for this assignment. In my heart I knew that was the truth. But I also believed that if the Lord had called me to do this, He would also equip me. I claimed the promise of Philippians 4:13 as my own: *"I can do all things through Christ who strengthens me."*

My letter writing ministry to this woman was a tedious endeavor. Each hand-written letter took a minimum of three mornings to compose. I couldn't even begin the letter until I had first immersed myself in prayer and pleaded with the Lord to speak to her through me. I was keenly aware that this woman didn't need to hear from me, but rather from the One who made her and loved her.

Day two consisted of writing the rough draft, and on day three I would polish the final letter and decorate it with stickers and drawings. A friend wisely encouraged me to copy each letter before sending it off and so I would traipse off to the office supply down the street to make a copy. I am so glad I took this advice because today I have 15 years of recorded memories as I have shared precious moments from my life with my friend.

My heart's desire was to minister to this woman, but I wasn't prepared for how my own life would be affected.

"Are you ready for this?"

I would think about her several times a day, wondering what she was doing and how she was feeling. I would be doing some ordinary task, such as cooking dinner or bathing a child and I would think, *She doesn't get to do this.* And I would say a silent prayer for my friend.

Sometimes I would be singing a song of praise to the Lord and wish I could teach it to my friend. Then there were times when I would think about her situation and my heart would spill down my cheeks. There were those other moments though when my heart would leap for joy when I read her letters and saw how much she was growing in Christ.

I sensed that the Lord desired to strengthen her through our relationship, but what I hadn't considered was how He would transform my heart and grow me as well. I began to understand a bit of what was meant by *"Are you ready for this?"* The Lord was drawing me into a deeper level of intimacy with Himself as I became more dependent upon Him. He was conquering areas of pride in me and teaching me about His unconditional love and acceptance.

I was learning to appreciate my own blessed life rather than grumbling when things didn't go my way. Holding my babies seemed a privilege and honor to me. Even cleaning house and doing laundry for my family were seen from a fresh perspective. All because I was willing to step out of my comfort zone in obedience to the Lord and reach out to a broken woman.

"Yes Lord; I *am* ready for this."

Candid Conversation Starters

1) Has God ever called you to do something uncomfortable? If so, what was it and how did you respond?

2) Read 1 Thessalonians 5:24. Do you believe God will accomplish everything He has called you to do? Do your actions back up that belief?

3) Do you ever take your own life for granted? Take a moment to think about all the little things you are thankful for.

4) If you were the only Christian someone ever met, would they want to get to know Jesus?

5) Is there another way you related to what Cheryl shared in this chapter? If so, what was it?

Baby Blues

Sheila Rhodes

"It's a girl!"

I had waited to hear those words for so long. It seemed so surreal when I finally heard them out loud. My obstetrician was so convinced I was having a little boy and I should name him Melvin Maynard. We would laugh about it as I went for my prenatal visits, but in my heart, I always knew it was going to be a little girl.

I had dreams of having natural childbirth, but God had a different plan. I wanted my husband beside me, so he could tell me to push and breathe, but due to toxemia (now known as pre-eclampsia) I had to have a cesarean section. At that point it didn't matter. All I wanted was a healthy baby.

After my stay in the hospital, I went home with my beautiful baby girl. She was perfect in every way with ten little fingers and ten little toes. She was bright-eyed and would follow my voice all over the room. I sang to her all the time before she was born, and even more afterward. I was so happy! But then the darkness started to creep in.

Everyone told me it was the "Baby Blues." I would cry

at anything and everything. I remember asking myself, *"How can I be so sad when God has given me this beautiful baby girl?"* Yet the darkness stayed, and I felt it deeply. I got to the point where I couldn't eat or sleep. I became so agitated at the tiniest things and I could feel my personality changing.

My mother knew something was different as she watched me slip into this dark depression. I was trying to fight it with everything I could, but I could feel myself slipping away. I went from being a joyful, happy person to an empty shell with no voice except the one in my head telling me what an unfit mother I was. The same voice kept telling me I shouldn't have had a baby, I didn't deserve to have her or I was going to hurt her.

My sweet husband tried to help me, but he didn't know how to help and I couldn't help myself. To make matters worse, I became physically sick and ended up having my gall bladder removed less than a month later. At first, I thought maybe my illness had made the Baby Blues worse and now things would get better, but that was not the case. I wasn't home long before they kicked back into high gear and that sense of worthlessness and hopelessness settled in even deeper.

I could no longer think rationally. My daughter was crying, and I heard the voice tell me, *"Just put the pillow over her face. No one will know."* It was at that point I yelled at God and told Him I wanted to die. I couldn't believe I could think such horrible thoughts. I had been a believer since I accepted Christ at the age of seven, yet now my faith was nowhere to be found. I was always praying, but now it was as if I didn't even exist in God's eyes.

I cried out to God and asked Him what I had done to make Him so angry with me. I had my Bible in my hand and

I threw it across the room. It was then that I finally heard His voice. I went over to pick it up and it this is what I read, *"The LORD your God in your midst, The Mighty One, will save; He will rejoice over you with gladness, He will quiet you with His love, He will rejoice over you with singing"* (Zephaniah 3:17).

I wept and wept. I was not forgotten. Over the next few weeks when I couldn't sleep or felt anxious, I would say this verse over and over. I even made it into a song that I would sing to myself and my daughter. The more I sang this song the less anxious and sad I felt.

I wish I could say my depression disappeared instantly, but it didn't. It lasted for five months. I remember the day the darkness broke like it was yesterday. I woke up, took a shower, and got dressed. This was a huge deal, as many days I just hadn't had the strength. In the afternoon I went to the bathroom to put makeup on. I looked in the mirror and thought *this doesn't look too bad*, and then did the other eye.

It was now February, the snow was melting, and the sun was shining. I put on some shoes, took my first steps outside the door into the light and walked to the mailbox with my baby girl. For the first time in months, I knew I was going to be okay.

This was thirty years ago. They didn't talk about post-partum depression (PPD) then and many still don't. I went to a doctor who told me all mothers go through this and I would get over it. I did, but it almost cost me my daughter's life as well as my own. I was blessed to have people who surrounded me with incredible love and a mom who never left me alone.

I never had any experience with depression before my pregnancy. I had no idea the depth to which PPD can take you, but I now have empathy and compassion for every mother who experiences it. No mother should have to suffer in silence or shame. If you have a daughter let her know so she can be aware of the symptoms, know the difference between Baby Blues and severe PPD, and seek treatment early. If you ever have feelings of sadness that last more than a week after giving birth, call your obstetrician and explain to her or him what is happening and how you are feeling.

Post-Partum Depression can hit any new mom. It doesn't depend on race, financial status or how much faith you have. It is something within the physical body. Hormones and their levels can cause women of all ages various health issues. The important thing to remember is you are not alone and there is nothing to be ashamed of in reaching out for help.

I may never know, and I am past the point of needing to understand why I had to go through it, but I do know this: We all have scars from various things which happen to us, but it is what we do with the scars that matters the most. Scars are reminders of what God has brought us through.

My prayer is for every woman to know how much she is valued and treasured by God, and that even in our darkest hours God is *always* with us.

Candid Conversation Starters

1) Do you struggle to understand your worth to Jesus? How would you describe your identity in Christ?

2) Read Psalm 51. Have you ever struggled with depression or known someone who has? Share your experience. And remember, it is okay to seek help. God never expects us to walk through anything alone.

3) Is there another way you related to what Sheila shared in this chapter? If so, what was it?

The Forgiveness Exercise

Laura Rath

> *"Be kind and compassionate to one another, forgiving each other, just as in Christ God forgave you."*
> ~ Ephesians 4:32 (NIV)

I didn't realize I had forgiven him. It's not that I didn't want to, I just hadn't noticed when it happened. I wasn't trying to forgive and forget. In fact, I wasn't thinking about it at all... until I found that old journal.

It was years ago when I had felt the hurt... the empty feeling of abandonment. We didn't see eye to eye on the severity of the situation, so for him it was over long ago. After all, it was one moment over a decade ago, but for some reason I couldn't let it go.

I carried it with me, year after year, letting it resurface long enough to drag me down into the emotional pain and anger again. I didn't plan to not forgive. I never yelled, "I will never forgive you for this." I just didn't think about the need to forgive, and therefore, couldn't get over it. I recognize that now.

Unforgiveness is a heavy burden to carry, but still I carried this grievance in my pocket, ready to whip out at a moment's notice.

It sounds ridiculous, doesn't it? Like I consciously planned when to wield my weapon of unforgiveness, and when to save it for another day. But I didn't think about it that way, or any way, really... because I had lost control.

Unforgiveness takes on a life of its own. It gets the upper hand and isn't afraid to assert its power. When we least expect it, unforgiveness comes alive and takes us back to the past where we can relive painful memories over and over, leaving us emotionally wrecked all over again.

Perhaps that's why God's Word speaks so often about forgiveness. God knows what it does to us. He knows how that seed of unforgiveness grows like a giant weed, taking over every part of our lives.

Last year, I came across a forgiveness exercise. To be honest, I didn't want to do it; I wanted to skip over it. However, as part of a group, I was going to encourage others to use the exercise, so I knew I couldn't not do it.

The exercise was to write down "I forgive _____ for _____," filling in the blanks with the person's name and wrong committed. Once one or more sentences were completed, it was time to pray, speaking each sentence out loud, giving it over to God, and asking for His help to forgive. This last part was to be done daily.

Using one of my journals, I reluctantly completed the exercise. Over the next few days, I prayed the forgiveness sentence out loud, asking for God's help to forgive and for the ability to move past it. Then I tucked the journal away out of sight and forgot about it. For over a year.

Not long ago, I pulled the same journal out of hiding, looking for something else I knew I had recorded there. As I flipped through the pages, I found my forgiveness sentence, which I had totally forgotten about. As I read what I wrote over a year ago, I was surprised to realize that I hadn't thought about it in months.

I had completely forgotten about the very grievance I had carried around for years. It no longer weighed on my shoulders. I remembered the incident, but this time it was without the pain. Without new tears. And without a rekindling of the anger that had always gone with it.

The forgiveness exercise worked, but not because of my own abilities. It worked because when I gave it to God, I had finally surrendered it to Him. I stopped trying to control the power it had over me, and I let God take control.

> *"For I will forgive their wickedness and will remember their sins no more."*
> ~ Hebrews 8:12 (NIV)

Seeing that sentence in my journal reminded me that God truly is at work even when I am not aware. I was no longer trying to forget the incident; I simply didn't remember it.

God does not need my help to forgive, but I definitely need His help to forgive others. Until I turned to God and asked for His help, I was unable to forget about what happened. For so many years, I let it hurt me. But once I surrendered it to Him, I was able to stop thinking about it. The grasp I had on it loosened and I didn't even feel it when God gently took it from me.

That is how He works… gently and when we are ready.

He wouldn't take from me what I wasn't prepared to give up. But when I was ready, God removed it, and in its place, I felt the healing that only forgiveness can bring.

Candid Conversation Starters

1) We have all struggled with forgiveness at one time or another. Can you think of a time you struggled to forgive someone, or someone you are struggling to forgive right now?

2) Do you recognize the importance of forgiveness? How would you describe it?

3) Read Luke 7:36-50. What stands out to you in those verses?

4) Is there another way you related to what Laura shared in this chapter? If so, what was it?

Stressed to the Max

Heather Hart

I didn't plan ahead. Well, I did. I planned to do four days of work in one morning.

It was a bad plan.

On the morning in question, I got multiple phone calls needing me to step out of my office and into other situations. Situations I couldn't say no to. Situations I *wouldn't* say no to. To top it all off, I was out of sugar to sweeten my morning coffee. I had issues to say the least.

In addition to my four days of work, I had planned to run to the store, make a costume for my daughter's school project, and take care of a whole slew of other tasks. Between basketball practice and dental appointments, my day was jam-packed from beginning to end.

One of my new tasks was picking up the yard before an unexpected rain shower. My mind was running a million miles a minute while I trudged around the yard picking up belongings that couldn't weather the storm. I wasn't upset with anyone but me. And while I would happily love and serve my family, a sense of panic was rising within.

I was silently beating myself up while trying to beat the storm.

Why didn't I plan better? Why wasn't I further ahead. Was I even qualified to do any of it? Was this really my calling? I obviously wasn't the best choice. Maybe God was trying to tell me something. Maybe He wanted me to hand off some of my projects or graciously step down from leading Bible study.

"For God so loved the world, that he gave his only Son, that whoever believes in him should not perish but have eternal life. For God did not send his Son into the world to condemn the world, but in order that the world might be saved through him."
~ John 3:16-17

How could you tell the difference between God's prompting and Satan's schemes anyways? Obviously, it wasn't dependent on my own opinions in the moment. What did God want from me?

And in the middle of my mess, I sensed that whisper deep within my soul. The one that could only be Jesus. The panic ceased, and I knew the answer was found in the gospel.

God loves me so much He sent His Son to live and die for me. And not just me, but everyone. I was created to bring Him glory. To shine His light to the world. That's what my ministry and obligations are truly about: pointing people to Jesus.

In the middle of my mess, I can do that because it's not about me. It's not about whether or not I have it all together. It isn't about whether or not I'm caught up, or have a good plan. It's about knowing we are all loved by God no matter where life finds us.

If you were to meet me in real life, or even visit my website and read through some of my blog posts, it would be obvious that I am a failure by the world's standards. Nobody would ever look at me and think #LifeGoals or even #SquadGoals. I'm better defined by #HotMess and #LifeHappens. But God doesn't pick out the perfect people to do His will. He doesn't stand back and wait for the cream of the crop to fight their way to the top and then send them on a mission for Him.

God calls the runts out of the field and makes them Kings (1 Samuel 16). He singles out the faithful, even if they are failures, and that is where I found myself that day. I had no idea how my morning would play out. I didn't know if I would get it all done. But I knew God was with me. I knew that I was unworthy, and I knew He called me anyway.

Maybe I just needed to step back for a moment and plug into God's Word. When Moses told God he was unworthy, when he questioned his calling, God didn't offer up reassurances, He just told Moses that He had it under control. It wasn't about Moses, it was about God (Exodus 3). And the same is true in my life and in my calling. It's not about me, it's about Jesus.

Candid Conversation Starters

1) Have you ever struggled with self-doubt that was based on your current situations instead of rooted in the truth of the gospel? Can you think of a specific time?

2) Read Isaiah 55:8. Do you believe that God is in control and that timing and plans are better than ours?

3) Have you ever needed to shift your focus from yourself to Jesus? What has helped you to do that, and how did it change your circumstance?

4) Is there another way you related to what Heather shared in this chapter? If so, what was it?

Where Does My Help Come From?

Lynn Landes

It comes every winter season, the dreaded stomach flu. Some seasons we are able to escape it, but in a family with young children, it seems inevitable. I can handle the mess, the fevers, body aches, runny noses, coughing, etc., but the suffering is what gets me every time. Every time one of them begs, "Help me, Mommy!" I can only weep inside as my heart breaks for what they are going through. It is a chasm in my soul that cannot be filled. Why not me? Let me do this for them?

My tears must not escape because they need me to be strong for them. Instead, I promise in soft, gentle whispers that, "I am here, you are not alone. It's going to be over soon." If I feel like this, I can't help but wonder how God must have felt watching Jesus suffer in those last few hours on Earth? As He cried out, *"My Father, if it is possible, do not give me this cup of suffering. But do what you want, not what I want"* (Matthew 26:39, NCV).

Jesus was calling out to His Father, feeling a separation from Him that He had never felt before. It was the beginning of His walk, where He carried humanity's sin. His suffering was just beginning, and I wonder who comforted God?

When Jesus cried out from the cross, *"My God, My God, Why have you forsaken me?"* (Matthew 27:46), how badly God must have wanted to protect Him and carry that burden for Him. His pain must have been indescribable. Indeed, in the final moments of His life it is written, *"And behold, the curtain of the temple was torn in two, from top to bottom. And the earth shook, and the rocks were split"* (Matthew 27:51).

Was this God's pain ricocheting across the Earth? That is a question that will be answered someday but it led me to other questions. Why, if Jesus knew the path He must walk, did He call out to His Father to save Him? After much study, I am beginning to understand that Jesus felt alone because He carried our sins for us.

Sin causes a separation from God and though He walked the Earth in human form, He had never been alone before. God was always with Him, yet in those last few days on Earth, Jesus had to walk as we, human sinners do. We walk through a world corrupted with sin, forever alone, unless we make the choice to give our life to God.

I know that while my children called out for me to help them, my soul was crying out to my Heavenly Father, who is always with me. He calms me, gives me the skills I need to take care of those entrusted to me during their time on this Earth, and I find that I am so thankful that I do not walk alone.

Now, after they finally fall asleep, my voice will cry out to my Father in gratitude for the lesson I have been given. "Thank You, thank You," I weep because I know I would not survive a moment more without His hand to guide me.

Candid Conversation Starters

1) What is one of your hardest struggles when it comes to everyday life as a Christian woman? Do you trust Jesus to help you through it?

2) Read 1 Corinthians 10:13. Do you believe that you aren't alone in your struggles? Is there something on your heart that you need to ask another believer to pray with you about?

3) Is there another way you related to what Lynn shared in this chapter? If so, what was it?

God is Faithful

Jaime Hampton

I have a soft spot in my heart for the disciple known as "Doubting Thomas." I think it's because he reminds me of myself. When I was little, my faith knew no bounds; I believed I could literally move mountains. When it didn't happen, it never occurred to me to wonder why, or to doubt God's existence; I just kept trying.

I think we are all born with pure, uncontaminated faith. But then something happens: that pure faith becomes contaminated by doubt. Maybe it comes in the form of a prayer that seems to go unanswered, or a situation that you can't reconcile with a loving God. It could be the attitudes or doubts of others that infect your faith. However it happens, most of us don't make it to adulthood without contracting the *disease of doubt*.

I personally got to a place in my teenage years where intellectual debates, questions, and arguments replaced the childlike faith I had always known. At one point during college, I found myself looking at other religions, wondering if I believed Christianity was true simply because I was raised in the church. If I am being totally candid with you, there are times that I still entertain those doubts to a certain degree.

In the doctor's office a few weeks ago I heard the word "benign" for the first time. I'd had a slow-growing lump in my armpit for the last few years, and wasn't expecting cancer, but hearing the word "benign" somehow shook me up more than getting the lump tested in the first place.

When faced with our mortality, when the rubber meets the road, do we really, honestly believe what the Bible says about God, Jesus, and eternal life? If we do have a solid belief in those things, are we fully convinced that we are not one of those who will cry, *"Lord, Lord!"* but be turned away with the heartbreaking response from Jesus, *"I never knew you"* (Matthew 7:21-23)?

Want to know something? *I wrestle with those doubts, too.* God knows it, so I am not afraid to admit it to you. Because I have experienced God's work in my life in ways that can't be explained otherwise, I always come back to a place of faith, no matter how far I stray, no matter how susceptible I am to the whispers of the Enemy. When the disease of doubt rears its ugly head in our spirits, we can research, debate, or read books until we are blue in the face, but in the end we need to experience God to come back to a place of belief. The same was true for our friend Thomas.

"Now Thomas (also known as Didymus), one of the Twelve, was not with the disciples when So the other disciples told him, 'We have seen the Lord!'

"But he said to them, 'Unless I see the nail marks in his hands and put my finger where the nails were,

and put my hand into his side, I will not believe.'

"A week later his disciples were in the house again, and Thomas was with them. Though the doors were locked,

Jesus came and stood among them and said, 'Peace be with you!' Then he said to Thomas, 'Put your finger here; see my hands. Reach out your hand and put it into my side. Stop doubting and believe.'

"Thomas said to him, 'My Lord and my God!'

"Then Jesus told him, 'Because you have seen me, you have believed; blessed are those who have not seen and yet have believed.'"

~ John 20:24-29 (NIV)

I really think he got a raw deal when he was given the nickname "Doubting Thomas." I think, in general, people look down their nose at Thomas because he didn't blindly believe that Jesus had appeared to the other disciples. But God gifts us with faith in different measures, and with a variety of gifts altogether. Of course, Jesus knew Thomas' gifts, and what he would require to come to a place of belief.

Romans 12:6 says, *"We have different gifts according to the grace given us. If someone's gift is prophecy, let him use it in proportion to his faith"* (NIV). And Romans 12:3 tells us, *"For through the grace given to me I say to everyone among you not to think more highly of himself than he ought to think; but to think so as to have sound judgment, as God has allotted to each a measure of faith"* (NIV).

If Thomas' need to see Jesus in the flesh was inherently wrong, it seems like Jesus would have appeared and responded immediately with a rebuke similar to the one He used many times with His disciples: *"You of little faith..."* But He doesn't. In fact, immediately after appearing and greeting the disciples, Jesus turns to Thomas, as if His appearance was primarily for Thomas' benefit, and says, *"Put your finger here; see my hands. Reach out your hand and put it into my side. Stop doubting and believe."* Instead of a rebuke, Jesus meets Thomas where he is, showing him the marks on His hands and side.

This act of experiencing God was a turning point for Thomas, and of course Jesus knew it would be. Jesus spoke life into him, saying *"Stop doubting and believe."* I don't know if this is as much *"go forth and sin no more,"* as it is "now I have created the conditions necessary for you to believe. Now you can stop doubting." Like telling the paralytic in John 5 to take up his mat and walk or sending the lepers in Luke 17 to the high priests, Jesus called Thomas into belief. **You could even say He healed him of the disease of doubt.** So, when I read this well-known story about Thomas, I don't see a negative example of a "doubter;" I see a positive picture of Jesus meeting us all right where we are.

My favorite part of this passage is Thomas' response to Jesus' appearance: *"My Lord and my God!"* This declaration of faith is one of, if not *the* most bold, heartfelt acknowledgments of Jesus' lordship recorded in Scripture. I don't think Thomas could have come to that place of total faith without first going through the time of doubting.

In fact, just as *"those who are forgiven much love much"* (Luke 7:47), I think sometimes those who don't come by their faith easily may have a greater passion behind that faith when it finally does come. Just as our immune systems become stronger after overcoming a pathogen, I believe that when our spirit is challenged by the disease of doubt, it grows stronger, and we emerge on the other side with a faith markedly more resistant to the same disease in the future. God uses the struggle as part of the journey, for His glory. When the struggle is there as the backdrop to the victory, the victory becomes all the sweeter, so much more valuable, driving our faith with all the more passion.

Are you struggling with doubts today? Are you living outwardly as if you had "blessed assurance," but inwardly feeling like a fraud? If so, I would urge you to confess those doubts to the Lord. Rob the Enemy of his power by approaching the throne of God just as Thomas approached Jesus: honestly; humbly. Remember God's promise that when we seek Him we will find Him, when we seek Him with all our hearts (Jeremiah 29:12-13).

If you find yourself struggling through a season of doubts, ask yourself if you are seeking God with all of your heart, or simply going through the motions of faith to gain worldly approval, to fit in with the church crowd. Call upon the Lord. Come, pray to Him—He will hear you! I know this because I have walked through seasons of doubt and am sure more will come. But seek Him with all of your heart, and you *will* find Him.

Jehovah Rapha, "Almighty God who heals you," will heal you of the disease of doubt. Your spirit will come out on the other side stronger for it, ready to take on the next challenge to your faith more quickly and empowered to live more boldly for the Lord—just like Thomas.

> *"Then you will call upon me and come and pray to me, and I will hear you. You will seek me and find me, when you seek me with all your heart.'*
>
> ~ Jeremiah 29:12-13 (NIV)

Candid Conversation Starters

1) What kind of doubts have you experienced as a Christian, or before you came to Christ?

2) Hebrews 4:12 says *"the Word of God is living and active,"* has God ever spoken to you at just the right moment through Scripture, an encouraging word from a friend, or in some other way? If so, how?

3) Is there another way you related to what Jaime shared in this chapter? If so, what was it?

Used and Abused

Alana Terry

He didn't rape me. That's what I told myself over and over whenever the distant memory surfaced. *It wasn't rape.* And if it wasn't rape, it wasn't a big deal, right?

I was newly married, enjoying my husband, looking forward to our brand-new life together. But somewhere in the back of my head was a recollection. A question.

Was I a victim?

The year before our wedding, I had worked at a home for troubled teens. I counseled girls who'd had horrible things done to them. I knew what real victims looked like. They didn't look like me. I was a ministry-minded Christian. A pastor's wife. My husband and I were raising money to become missionaries. My goal was to make the Proverbs 31 woman jealous. And since he hadn't raped me, I couldn't be a victim.

Then came more questions stemming from that event in my distant past. *If I wasn't a victim, why did I feel so ashamed? If what I went through wasn't abuse, why did I keep thinking about it?*

I knew I hadn't been raped. It wasn't as if I questioned my own memories of the situation. My memory was working quite well, if not a little over zealously. I knew exactly what he had done, when he had done it, and how he had done it. Nothing was blocked out like it would have been if I were *really* victimized.

I was a kid. He was a teen. It was basically innocent, wasn't it? And even if it wasn't, stuff like that happens all the time. *Experimentation*, or whatever label folks want to throw on it.

It wasn't rape. Which meant it wasn't abuse. Which meant I wasn't a victim.

So why was I on the phone crying with my mentor from the girls' home? Why was I explaining to her in embarrassingly vivid detail exactly what it was that happened to me so many years ago?

"You have a question for me, don't you?" Beth asked when I was done.

I hemmed and hawed like a donkey with a bellyache.

"Is there something you wanted to ask?"

I bit my lip. I bit my nails. I probably bit my tongue. And then I finally managed to stammer, "So, what *was* that?"

I was at the point in my life when I needed to heal. Needed to grow. But something held me back; until I could put a label onto this awkward, shameful, not-so-very-innocent thing that had been done to me when I was still a child, I couldn't move forward.

"What do you mean?" Beth prodded like a nurse digging her scalpel beneath the skin to pull out that blood-covered sliver.

She was going to make me say the word, wasn't she? Okay. I was a big girl now. I could do it. "Was that abuse?" I asked, making sure to add a little giggle afterward so I could always pretend I was joking if she guffawed at my naiveté.

But Beth didn't guffaw. "What would you say if one of the girls here asked you that same question about something that happened to them?"

Well, in that case it was so simple, "I'd tell them it was abuse."

"Even though it wasn't rape?" There she went again, using that horrid vocabulary I wanted to avoid.

"Yeah."

And then Beth said what I'd already come to realize. "Well, there's your answer."

And so, at the ripe old age of twenty-one, I came to understand I was the victim of childhood sexual abuse. I read a few books. Talked it out with Beth a few more times. And then I learned to move on. Learned to heal.

One in three women in our country are victims of sexual abuse. In some places, like where I live in rural Alaska, upwards of eighty percent of children (boys and girls) are sexually abused. I know I'm not alone. But I also know that I don't need to hide behind excuses anymore.

But he didn't rape me.

But stuff like that happens all the time.

But it could have been so much worse.

I am a survivor of sexual abuse. And I am one of the lucky ones. It is not something I think about day to day. It's not something that defines me or my sexuality. Not everybody has it so easy. But the fact that my experience with abuse was so "easy" compared to others meant that it took me over a decade to admit to myself that what I went through truly was wrong. It was sinful. It was unjustifiable on any moral level.

It wasn't until that point where I found true healing.

If you have experienced sexual abuse in any form—from lewd or suggestive remarks to inappropriate touching to forced sexual activity—you are not alone. You are not guilty. You are not defiled.

> *"The Spirit of the Lord is upon me, because he has anointed me to proclaim good news to the poor. He has sent me to proclaim liberty to the captives and recovering of sight to the blind, to set at liberty those who are oppressed, to proclaim the year of the Lord's favor.'*
>
> ~ Luke 4:18-19

The God who healed in Bible times is active today in the lives of His precious children. We are cleansed. We are whole. But sometimes it takes longer than others for us to experience that healing and restoration.

May you rest in His purity today. May you experience the cleansing, healing, and redemption that comes from the deep and unending love of our Heavenly Father.

Addendum

The National Clearinghouse on Family Violence reports that 55% of North Americans are victims of sexual abuse.[3] That's over half of our population. Of that number, they report that one out of every three female children will be

---

[3] Abuse Statistics - The Statistics On Abuse. Anxietycentre.com. Accessed February 28, 2018. http://www.anxietycentre.com/abuse-statistics-information.shtml

sexually abused or assaulted before they reach the age of 18.[4] But sexual abuse is only one type of abuse. Abuse can come in many different forms and happen at any age. Here are some of the different categories of abuse:

- Physical abuse
- Sexual abuse
- Neglect
- Verbal abuse
- Psychological abuse

Please know that God cares about you and what you are going through, no matter what it is labeled or how severe it is.

Candid Conversation Starters

1) Have you ever been hurt or abused? Were you able to move forward from that? If so, how?

2) What do Scriptures like Psalm 18:2, 28:8, 36:7, and Romans 8:1 remind us of?

3) Is there another way you related to what Alana shared in this chapter? If so, what was it?

---

[4] Ibid.

Seeing With Your Heart

Janet Perez Eckles

My "careless" driving became the joke of the neighborhood. Three times I had backed into the mailbox at the end of our driveway. With gritted teeth and red cheeks, I gave another excuse. Each one covered the real reason: I simply didn't see it.

"Yes, your retina is deteriorating," the ophthalmologist had said months earlier. He paused, then added, "You need to prepare. There is no cure, and no one knows how long you'll have your sight."

By the time I reached thirty, my life had turned out better than a storybook. My husband's quick climb up the corporate ladder brought a special gift for me—the ability to stay home with my little ones. I took care of our three sons with delight and sighed with contentment at our perfect life— a life paved with success and prosperity.

Until one day, my world began to shake. While my three, five, and seven-year-old sons wiggled in the back seat, I drove down a familiar street near our home. I turned my blinker, glanced to the side before changing lanes. And unexpectedly, a loud metal clunk to my left startled me. Heart thumping, I glanced to see the car I had sideswiped. It had come from nowhere. With the same shock, the effects of the retinal disease scraped pain into my life.

The bleak news from the ophthalmologist hovered over my sleepless nights. First I experienced night blindness, next my peripheral vision began to close in. I fought the notion I was losing my sight, but the evidence fought back emphasizing the inevitable blindness that awaited me.

During nap time, I would kneel beside my youngest son's bed as he slept. And with tears burning my eyes, I stared at his features—his long eyelashes resting on his chubby cheeks, his dark hair strands slipping down on his forehead, and his lips that resembled his Dad's. I engraved that image in my heart.

A few short months swept by, along with more of my sight. I could only see what one sees through a keyhole. Struggling to see the phone book, I searched for specialists, healers, herbal treatments. I inquired about transplants, even experimental developments in foreign countries. Adding to my anxiety, all gave negative answers.

Though I wanted to stay positive, I couldn't. I was losing something I valued, something vital for my survival, and I was losing it way too quickly. Finally, the day came when the faint light I saw turned to a dark gray nothing. And the prognosis that I would be blind the rest of my life made me tremble.

For weeks, I had cried out to God, prayed and begged umpteen times. With a wrinkled tissue in hand, I had dabbed my tears. Then held my breath and in the silence, I heard the rumbling of my sons in the other room. Their world hadn't changed, but mine had been turned upside down.

What I didn't know was that God's love was also turning to answer my prayers. A friend invited me to her Christian church where I found the answer. It came in one single Bible verse. In Matthew 6:33 (NIV), God said, *"...seek first his kingdom and his righteousness, and all these things will be given to you as well."*

Seek Him first? I had been seeking to see again, to have a normal life, and to care for my sons. That was my number one priority.

But the more that Bible verse resonated in me, the more my heart softened. I made a silent decision to obey. I sought God first by listening to the Bible on audio, day after day, week after week, and God's Word covered my soul. Eventually, everything changed. Fear vanished. Insecurities left. And wisdom and strength filled me.

My spiritual eyes opened for me to see what truly mattered, what gave me joy, what brought meaning to my life.

And what increased my passion was knowing my limitations hadn't changed my role as a mom, nor altered my contribution to our marriage. I was still the same inside, sightless, but with more determination to care for my family. I was unable to walk on my own, but God helped me navigate through life.

I vowed then, to focus on the needs of my boys, to seek ways to still be their mom and not to shuffle through life, but instead, take sure, firm steps while holding the banner of God's victory.

One evening I came home from a prayer meeting. "Hey guys," I greeted them, "I'm home. Did you behave for Daddy?" I tossed my purse on the couch and scooped my three-year-old, Joe into my arms, "I need a big hug."

"Need some help?" My husband offered.

"Nope, I'm home, and I'll take over," I assured him. "Come on, all of you, its bath time." I rounded them up.

Instinctively, I counted the steps down the hallway and felt for the banister to head upstairs.

Once in their bedrooms, I pulled out their one-piece pajamas from their dresser drawer. I reached in the bathroom closet for towels and groped to find the soap in the tub.

While all three giggled and teased each other, in a matter-of-fact tone, my three -year-old said, "Mom has eyes at the end of her fingers."

I smiled at his unique reasoning. He was right. My fingertips became my eyes—the effective sensors transforming what I touched into clear images in my mind. My hearing sharpened also. I could differentiate their every sound, one voice from the other. I recognized each utterance—from their rambunctious screams to their faint whimpers.

And each time they attempted to "trick Mom" by eating treats before meals, my sense of smell tracked any aroma wafting from their direction. Each trick they pulled became an opportunity to teach them to laugh and to embrace a sense of humor.

Learning to see with my heart, life became beautiful again. We gather with neighbors who understand my limitations. And I in turn, understand the richness of life when one chooses to see beyond the obstacles. That is when we find joy in what's true. We look to what is best, and count on what brings peace to the soul.

Candid Conversation Starters

1) Have you ever let an inability or insecurity define your worth? If so, what was it?

2) Do you evaluate your life the way the world would, or do you try to see it from God's perspective?

3) Song of Solomon 4:7 says that *"there is no flaw in you."* Do you believe that? See also Psalm 27:4, Genesis 1:26, Psalm 45:11, and Zephaniah 3:17.

4) Is there another way you related to what Janet shared in this chapter? If so, what was it?

Letting Go of Unforgiveness

Stephanie M. Carter

Unforgiveness is a cancer to your soul that will bring torment and pain beyond the original offense committed against you. How do I know? I lived it.

I have found that we all have some sort of struggle that we either face now or will face in the future. My struggle was with unforgiveness. There are others, but I am addressing this particular one here. I am not ashamed to admit it and if you struggle with it, you need to not be ashamed either. But, we do need to deal with it head on.

At the time of my well justified, unforgiving heart condition (so I thought), I was hurting from a transgression that I believed had nothing to do with me needing to forgive. I justified it based on the level of the transgression. I had my rights. I was done wrong! Oh, and I need to mention, I held this belief as a Christian.

I am sure that many of you reading this have had an offense committed against you that you found extremely difficult to forgive. You may have even been like me and just flat out refused to forgive at first. The other person was wrong, and you did nothing so why do you need to forgive.

Not many years ago, I was in a great marriage. I married my best friend and felt I had married the man of my dreams. I loved him deeply and actually felt I had won the lottery when we married in June of 1992. I was a happy woman. I was an over the top thrilled married woman. I loved marriage. I loved my husband and everything about starting a life with him, starting a family. I trusted him.

We were both Christians when we married, and I felt totally safe and secure with him. Until, one day, I found out that the man I was married to was in an affair and a child was resulting from it. I felt my world crash down around me. It felt like my world was burning up. Our dreams were up in flames.

"I was devastated," didn't come close to describing how I felt. Depression lay on my soul like a heavy slab of concrete. Anger burned in my heart. The hurt was overwhelming. Malice was looked upon as a friend. Loneliness was my companion. Fear gripped my emotions. Insecurity was filling every thought. Confusion was endless and suicide thoughts were an inviting and welcomed idea.

Worse than all that, I couldn't forgive. I wouldn't forgive. I didn't feel I needed to. Why should I? He and the mistress did this to me.

But, how many of you know that God always comes after us? Think about it. Most of the time we are not looking for God when we are in our place of pain, darkness, or deception, but somehow, God finds us. He reaches out His loving hand and grace and does what only He can do: He gets our attention and saves us from ourselves.

When I was so unwilling to forgive at first, it was not easy. I was taken to the story in Matthew 18 where Peter wanted to know how many times he should forgive someone. Jesus' reply to him was a parable about a king and his servants. A servant owed a huge debt that he could never repay, and the king forgave it after his servant begged for time to repay it. Well, it was a debt that was really worth, in time, 150,000 years. He could never repay that. But the king had compassion and released him of the debt.

Then, this same servant went right out and found someone that owed him money, in a much smaller amount. The amount equivalent to one day's wage. Now that was payable. Yet, this same forgiven servant took this man that owed one day's wage and choked him and demanded the debt be paid to him.

How quickly we forget right? Well, the king found out what he was doing, and that forgiven servant found himself before the king again and was sent to the tormentors for his unforgiveness. He was even called wicked.

Now the most important part of this story, as the Bible records, is that Jesus said that if you and I do not forgive from our hearts, our Heavenly Father will do the same to us. What "same to us?" He will turn us over to the tormentors. You see, God expects forgiven people to forgive others; so much so that He connects His forgiveness with ours.

Wow! Who wants to be tormented? I certainly don't. It is sobering when you think about it.

Forgiveness is not dependent on the level of offense committed against you. No matter how small or large the offense is, we are required by God to forgive. Why? Because God, sent Jesus to die and shed His blood for us. Jesus was made the propitiation for our sin. (Propitiation is just a fancy word meaning satisfaction.) Jesus was the perfect sacrifice. He satisfied the requirement necessary to pay our debt of sin.

A debt we would could never repay because we, as sinners, had no way of repaying it. We were not the perfect sacrifice. It was unpayable by us.

Because of what Jesus did, we are forever, always, already forgiven. Even if we do not walk in it. But we must appropriate it in our daily lives. When we don't, we say that the blood of Jesus was not enough for our sins.

When we do this, we invalidate the blood sacrifice in our own lives. We come under torment. The blood of Jesus covers all sin including the ones committed by me, but also against me and you. The torment I felt was in the form of depression, anger, malice, sadness, grief, hurt, and more.

After holding my unforgiveness for my husband and the mistress for about four years, I could take no more. I had to get free. I write about that freedom in my book, *Tomorrow Is Not Promised.* I tell in one chapter how I got free from that horrible justifying sin in my heart.

The day came when I attended a Forgiving Forward conference and I soon realized after the speaker gave his address that I had not truly forgiven, even though I said I had with my lips. My heart was angry. I felt I had the right to be angry. Who wouldn't? I suffered a lot. I based my unforgiveness on the level of pain I felt and the infraction my husband and mistress committed. I truly could not bless them and wish they had no consequences.

But the day came when I couldn't take it anymore. I knew that if I didn't forgive I would come under torment. No, I was already under torment but was just telling myself I wasn't. I told myself all sorts of things to keep my sin justified: "It was his fault, he needs to forgive." "They ruined my life." "She is so wrong." "They knew better." "I didn't ask for this why should I forgive."

I drove about 45 minutes away to see a forgiveness counselor who led me in a three-to-four-hour session of walking through forgiveness that set me free. I was finally able to totally forgive my husband for all he had done. Never to bring it up to him again. A week or so later I forgave the mistress. Was it hard? Yes. Was it worth it? Immensely.

God loves you and me so much that He never stops dealing with our hearts. He will never let us go. No matter what we have done forgiveness is ours. But, the amazing thing is that forgiveness is not just for us, but for all the sins committed against us by others and any sin committed in the past, present, and future.

Have my ex-husband and his mistress repented and said they are sorry to me? No, they have not. Do I need that anymore? Not really. It is not that important. My freedom is far more important than imprisoning myself with the torment that comes with unforgiveness.

Forgiveness doesn't make what a person has done to you right, it just makes you free. God has done all He can do. The satisfaction has been met for your sin and anyone who sins against you. If you are holding unforgiveness today, let it go.

One, last story. I am now a forgiveness coach with the same ministry that helped me get free. I recently did a session with a woman who needed to forgive someone for murdering her teenage son over ten years ago. After three hours with me, she was able to forgive this man. Until that time, her whole life was on hold. She lived in pain every day of her life. She was filled with the torment of anger, hurt, bitterness, grief, and depression. Within a matter of three hours she was free from her prison. When you don't forgive, you don't put the other person in prison, you put yourself in one. A prison that Jesus says you have the key to, and that key is forgiveness.

Receive that gift today and become free. Live your life the way God intended. It is there for the taking. Be free.

Candid Conversation Starters

1) Have you ever tried to justify unforgiveness? If so, how?

2) Read James 2:14-26; Colossians 3:12-14; Hebrews 12:14-15; 1 John 3:16; and Matthew 6:33. What is the danger of unforgiveness, and how can we learn to let it go?

3) Is there another way you related to what Stephanie shared in this chapter? If so, what was it?

She Did What She Could

Rebecca Hastings

I stood in front of the graves. His and hers, cracked and covered in light moss, yet they were still clear enough to read.

He did what he set out to do.

She did what she could.

I shook my head in disbelief. How is this possible? How could she be that person? The dates on the graves didn't matter to me. I stood dumbfounded at the injustice of a life half lived, not in years but in purpose.

I long to be a person of purpose. The kind of person who gets things done, who accomplishes what she sets out to do. I want to storm the world for the Kingdom of God, but here I am doing laundry and signing permission slips, grocery shopping and driving carpool. It's the life I chose, but it seems far too ordinary for Kingdom work. And I fear I have become what was on her gravestone: *She did what she could.*

This is the place where I am sure I'm doing something wrong. Certain I am not good enough, doing enough, godly enough. And here is where I wonder if I will ever be enough.

Have you been there? Looking around I see the shiny

people on the internet living out purpose, doing God's work. Clearly, they have something figured out that I haven't gotten a handle on.

Maybe it is the person traveling from mission field to mission field capturing hearts and feeding bellies. I watch and think how much I would love to be there serving a starving people and really living for God.

Or the woman on the stage who preaches truth like an arrow to hearts. She's got a direct line to God and she knows exactly what to do with it. Plus, she's got great hair.

And then there is the woman who seems like me until she isn't. She is the perfect wife and mother, finding time to serve in her church, her community, and her family. You know the ones with the matching outfits and squeaky-clean smiles.

I look around and see all these women with purpose, living out exactly what they are called to. They walk forward in boldness loudly declaring the name of Jesus while I sit here with a basket of mismatched socks whispering God's name like a question.

And I do what I can, all the while feeling like I have failed. ***But what if that's enough?*** What if we are not all meant for big, bold, spotlight service?

Remember the widow and her offering in Mark 12?

"Sitting across from the offering box, he [Jesus] was observing how the crowd tossed money in for the collection. Many of the rich were making large contributions. One poor widow came up and put in two small coins—a measly two cents. Jesus called his

> *disciples over and said, 'The truth is that this poor widow gave more to the collection than all the others put together. All the others gave what they'll never miss; she gave extravagantly what she couldn't afford—she gave her all.''*
>
> ~ Mark 12:41-44 (MSG)

There was a crowd, a space full of people. Some were clamoring to get to that offering box. Some probably held back. Rich person after rich person came and tossed in large amounts of money. But the widow didn't have much to give... Just two small coins.

 I wonder how she felt standing in that crowd. Money wasn't as easy to carry then, and surely her lack was noticeable. Did she feel plain and ordinary next to these people who gave so much? Did she lack purpose just because her offering was small?

She didn't let her feelings stop her. She went up, bold or on shaky knees, and gave all she had. She took what was before her and gave it all to God. She gave fully, and Jesus commended her for it. He noticed her in all of her ordinary smallness. Isn't that what we are all silently begging for?

The carved words from those two gravestones whisper deep into the back of my mind, and I can't help but wonder if maybe I have got this all wrong. Maybe we are more like the widow than we think.

"He did what he set out to do" exudes strength and boldness. But strength in who? Boldness in what? Having purpose without Jesus is like having riches and offering only a part.

She did things differently. This wasn't about her. This was about what was placed before her. She looked it all over, took it in and did what she could. She didn't try to be more than she was supposed to. She didn't seek praise or complain that the others had it so much easier. She simply took all she was given and did all she could.

When we see the choice before us, it becomes easier to see our true purpose. God doesn't call us to pave our own way. Our purpose is woven into all the things He places before us. When we do those things faithfully we honor God and the calling on our lives.

What is God placing before you right now? Is it a family and household to run or a job you may be less than excited about? Is it a sick parent or a friend who is hurting? Is it simply a basket of mismatched socks and dinner on the stove?

Whatever is before us today, may we learn to give ourselves fully to God in that place. May we lay aside purpose statements and bold declarations to simply find Jesus in whatever He has put before us. And may we be women who can say before the Father, I did what I could.

Candid Conversation Starters

1) Do you care more about getting things done, or about committing your life and actions to Christ, even in the small things?

2) Do you ever let the success of others make you feel less accomplished, unworthy, or lacking? How should 1 Corinthians 12 change the way we look at other women?

3) Is there another way you related to what Becky shared in this chapter? If so, what was it?

More Than Worry

Joi Copeland

In January of 2009, my husband and I noticed his grandfather wasn't acting normal. We didn't think a lot about it, due to him missing his deceased wife. We received a phone call a week later saying he passed out. After tests, we discovered he had cancer and it reached his brain.

We took our three boys to the hospital, ages six, five, and four. That is when it happened. My heart began to flutter as we left the hospital. I couldn't feel my arm and started freaking out. We dropped our boys off at a friend's house and went to a different emergency room. They ran a series of tests. No heart issues, but anxiety had instilled itself in me.

That year, after Grandpa passed away, we moved to Colorado. The anxiety had been kept at bay, which was great for me. We moved to Lakewood, and after a time, I started having anxiety attacks again. The debilitating kind where you cannot function. I had people tell me to pray, and I would get better, that I wasn't trusting in God enough with my problems. Those people meant well, but it ended up hurting my relationship with God. I stopped praying and reading the

Bible, because I obviously didn't trust Him enough or I wouldn't have anxiety.

I had some amazing people in my life who sat with me, watched my kids for me. My dad came out and stayed with me for ten days. I was finally getting better. I began driving without fear again. I was able to function. My relationship with Jesus suffered, though. I couldn't understand why He allowed this. But after a time, we "made up".

In 2012, we bought a house in Lakewood. In June, my anxiety came back in full force. This time, it was so bad I couldn't stop crying. I didn't turn from God this time, though. No, I came before Him, as 1 Peter 5:7 says, *"casting all your cares upon Him for He cares for you."* I laid in bed, tears streaming down my face, casting these deep cares on Him. I knew God cared for me then, and still cares for me now.

My husband and I had a huge discussion about going to the doctor. Something more than fear was going on, and the doctor confirmed that. I am now on anxiety medication. I used to be ashamed of that. But after talking with some amazing people, they encouraged me, telling me if I had cancer, I would take medicine to get well. It is the same thing with anxiety.

I have nothing to be ashamed of. If you are struggling with depression or anxiety, talk to your doctor. It could be something more than just worry. Because anxiety and worry are not the same thing and should never be treated as such.

May God bless you in all you do as you follow Him!

Candid Conversation Starters

1) Do you believe that God can handle your burdens?

2) Read Psalm 103, does anything stand out to you in that passage?

3) Is there another way you related to what Joi shared in this chapter? If so, what was it?

Dealing With Loss

Sherry Chamblee

Years ago, when I was a young wife and mom with three kids, living in southern California, I found out I was pregnant again. I had already experienced a miscarriage at the beginning of that year, so this pregnancy was a blessing.

I was about 22 weeks along when, one Sunday night, the pastor preached a sermon on the grace of God. Over and over again that night he said, "God will take care of you." He even broke into song, singing an old hymn with the phrase in it. Afterwards, people were remarking about how adamant the pastor was in this sermon, about how earnest and urgent he seemed to be to get it through to us that God will indeed take care of us, and that His grace is sufficient through everything.

The next morning, I went in to the OB-GYN to have a routine check-up on my pregnancy. My husband couldn't go with me, so I had a friend waiting in the lobby for me instead. I remember going in to the doctor, and they took out the instruments to hear the baby's heartbeat.

Only they couldn't find one.

My doctor became very concerned, and I remember

having such a feeling of dread come over me. I knew something wasn't right. The doctor was very serious when she took me aside and told me the truth: she couldn't find a heartbeat, and she feared that the baby was lost. She wanted to be sure though, so she ordered an advanced imaging procedure. I was to go to another facility right away and have it done.

Both my dear friend and I were shaken, but she bravely drove me to the other facility and sat alone in the waiting room again while I endured a 45-minute procedure—an in-depth scan of the baby. The technician was silent, and she did not turn the monitor toward me. I knew it was not what I had hoped. I knew the doctor wasn't wrong.

We went back to my OB and she looked over the results. The baby was definitely gone, plus I was farther along than the baby had developed. The baby was only at about the size of a 19-week-old gestation.

This was devastating. I was devastated. I was numb.

The doctor wanted to perform an induction, because I was going through absolutely no signs of labor at all, yet the baby had probably been gone for three weeks. Unfortunately, there were no beds available at the local hospital until Thursday, so I was going to have to wait in that state for the rest of the week.

Thus began the longest week of my life. I went to the Ladies' Bible study Tuesday morning, physically showing that I was pregnant but knowing the truth. Somehow a couple ladies of the church knew what was going on—to this day I can't imagine how they knew, except that my husband must have called someone from our church and told them. But it was a large church, and many ladies did not know.

I remember one very sweet lady at the Bible study asked

when I was due, and I nearly passed out from the shock of the question. Someone at our table told her, I don't remember who, and I don't remember the conversation. She felt bad, and part of me wishes I would have stayed home from that Bible study just to avoid the awkward moment for both of us. But one thing that had been drilled into me over the year or two before was how important it was to stay in a good church attendance routine when going through a trial. I needed to press on and stay connected, so I went on Tuesday. And I went again that Wednesday night to our church's prayer service (though I arrived at the last minute and sat in the back, hoping no one would notice me).

It was then, when the pastor got up to preach, that I remembered the sermon from the previous Sunday night. I don't know what he preached on that Wednesday, but I relived the Sunday night service from a few days before, as if he were preaching it live all over again. I heard him saying over and over that God's grace would take care of me, and I heard him singing the song.

I still felt numb, I still felt powerless, but suddenly I felt wrapped in a bubble. The rest of the world was tilting out of control, but I sat still and let it spin because I wasn't moving. There is almost no way to describe it in words, and over the years since then I have tried, but this sense of being on the inside of an invisible bubble of stability is the best and closest I can come to what it was like.

God's grace, given to me when I needed it most, was holding me still and secure, and it kept holding me through the rest of that night, and into the hospital the next day, through that terrible labor and seeing my baby boy resting peacefully in my arms. He was already with God in Heaven, I knew that, but I could feel God's arms around me too. Not like physical arms, but like a protective force field in which I could not be moved.

The things I had read in the Bible about God's grace suddenly became alive like never before. I wouldn't wish something like this upon myself again, nor anyone else, but it was such an amazing thing to experience God's grace in that way.

I write all this hoping to let others know that God's grace is just as available for you as it was for me, and that He gives it freely when His child needs it. No matter what you may go through, God's grace is there for you like nothing else.

No matter what is happening, please know that if you are His child, He has you wrapped up in an invisible force field of His grace, and that you—who you are on the inside— cannot be moved out of His care.

Candid Conversation Starters

1) Do you trust that God will take care of you no matter what you are going through? Is there a time when you remember leaning into Him in a whole new way?

2) In Psalm 77, Asaph was recounting the deeds of the Lord and remembering some of the good things He had done in the past. Can you remember some of the ways you have seen God work for good in your life?

3) Is there another way you related to what Sherry shared in this chapter? If so, what was it?

God Is In Control

Mary C. Findley

For about eight years, I rode shotgun in an 18-wheeler alongside my husband, Michael, who is an over the road tractor trailer driver. We visited the 48 continental states multiple times and all the Canadian provinces at least once. Our last truck was our home fulltime aside from occasionally staying with our daughter in her apartment.

We got to see some beautiful scenery and terrible weather. We got to listen to truck music (the sound of the wind blowing through trailers in a parking lot is kind of like organ pipes). We used a different bathroom almost every day.

We did everything from publishing books to fighting off monster colds while picking up and delivering all kinds of loads. From paper plates to pretty scary hazmat stuff to potatoes, we hauled it all. I started riding with Michael just after our youngest son graduated high school and went into the Army.

This January our third truck blew its engine. We were unable to finance repairs or a replacement truck, so now Michael is driving for a company and I am living with our daughter. It might seem strange, but the transition back to a "normal" life with an apartment, a job, and even, strange as it may seem, regular church membership and attendance, has been difficult.

While on the road, we tried to attend truck stop chapels whenever there was one to go to. But it's a tough ministry and fewer and fewer drivers care to attend. We heard all kinds of presentations, but we are grateful for those who cared enough to try to minister to those of us who couldn't quite fit our 72-foot-long everyday transportation into a church parking lot.

My life verse is Proverbs 16:3: *"Commit thy works unto the Lord, and thy thoughts shall be established"* (KJV). Over and over through these past years, in the truck, and transitioning back off the road, I have had trouble with clarity and concentration. I need to focus to get things done. I thought it was hard in the truck where there is a lot of noise and many distractions. I had to help my husband with phone calls to agents, brokers, shippers, and receivers, plus juggle paperwork (think eight years without a table). But it is even harder these days, mentally, physically, and spiritually.

I have told people I feel like I am back to Christianity 101. What is God's will for our lives? We know we are to continue writing (fiction and nonfiction to entice readers to draw closer to God and His Word). We are writing homeschool curriculum in the hope that we can help restore the foundation of true world history, science, and literature that builds people up. And we hope to get back to making videos for our visually-oriented society.

My husband is experiencing some health challenges and doesn't think he can keep driving for very many more years. His income is the main support for our plans to settle down eventually. We recently bought our first car in about ten years, and we are building a home in Oklahoma near our daughter and some of my husband's family. We are just following steps the Lord seems to be leading us to take and believing He will provide.

We are not exactly Abraham and Sarah, going we know not where, but maybe the challenge is to let God lead, step by step, committing our works to the Lord, and letting Him establish our thoughts and plans. I used to think that would happen in a snap, but maybe we would get proud of our own accomplishments if things just fell into place and worked immediately. Maybe that is the lesson God wants us to learn. Just the same way we would deliver one load with the truck and start looking for another, we may just have to do this step by step.

Another Scripture says, *"hitherto hath the Lord helped us"* (1 Samuel 7:12, KJV). Step by step, all along the way, we have weathered storms, just like the time we stayed three days in a truck stop with the trucks all getting buried in snow and ice and the restaurant cook not even being able to get in. But some people were stranded out on the interstate or over at a shopping mall with no overnight facilities or showers. Little by little, day by day, the snow subsided, and plows and tow trucks got the trucks free.

So, I think the key is remembering God is in control. Maybe not the way we expect or hope or plan, but He does have a plan. Moses couldn't see God's plan trudging along with those grumblers in the wilderness, but God led them, step by step. And His Word is there to lead us, step by step.

I once heard a devotional where the speaker said she studied the book of Judges and kept saying, "How could they keep doing evil in the sight of the Lord?" Then she put her own name in place of "The Children of Israel." Doing so brought home the fact that we are all complainers, sinners, and wrongdoers. Maybe the path God is trying to lead us along is littered with our own stumbling blocks. But I am hoping that part of the clarity and concentration I pray for includes clearly seeing God, His holiness, and His Spirit's leading. And that I won't be the guy in the cartoon based on the poem *Footsteps* where Jesus says, "And you see those grooves? That's where I dragged you, kicking and screaming."

Candid Conversation Starters

1) Do you struggle to commit your works to the Lord?

2) Do you believe that God is in control, no matter what happens?

3) What comfort can we draw from Luke 12:22-26 and Isaiah 41:10?

4) Is there another way you related to what Mary shared in this chapter? If so, what was it?

Overwhelmed

Dr. Karen Michelle Ricci

Our world is so fast paced these days. It seems like everyone and everything is constantly *Go! Go!! Go!!!* Some people even brag about how packed their schedule is. They crave being busy.

The end result, however, is compounded stress and tension in our daily lives. Of course, whether you are stuck in the busyness of life or not, "adulting" is something that none of us can get away from. It seems the fires we have to put out, and the decisions we have to make, are never ending. This can easily cause strain at times. It often feels like we are walking a tension-filled tightrope, of sorts.

There is tension between home and anything we do outside the home, as we strive to balance out the two. There is tension between making sure our marriage flourishes but, at the same time, we have to make sure our children's needs are met. A simple trip to the grocery store could even become tense if you happen to get stuck in traffic or end up with a grumpy cashier.

Not to mention how quickly our lives could fall into a

tail spin if something unexpected pops up: a health crisis, we lose a loved one, or maybe we lose a job. When left to our own devices, the hard times and tension of life can become unbearable. Like it or not, our earthly lives are full of moments that can cause our flesh to just feel plain... uncomfortable.

Have you ever thought about how, not only do we have to deal with earthly tension, but how, as believers in Jesus, we also have to deal with divine tension? Think about it. Our lives, as children of God, are full of dichotomies—truths that almost seem to be, not only opposite but, almost at odds with each other. God lifts up the humble but brings low the proud. If we want to be "great" in the Kingdom, then we need to be a servant. The Kingdom is now, but it is also "to come." And the list could go on and on.

Almost as far back as I can remember, my life has been full of tension and challenges. At age nine, I was diagnosed with a very aggressive autoimmune disease (juvenile rheumatoid arthritis). This caused a lot of physical pain and damage to the joints in my small frame. Even in my youth, I began to feel the divine tension between Heaven and Earth. My favorite Bible stories, growing up, were the ones where Jesus was healing people. He even brought people back to life! So, I knew He could heal me. But, for whatever reason, it hadn't happened yet.

"*Why?* Is this a test?" I would cry out to God. My faith in God was not lost, but I did have unanswered questions. I did my best, on my own, to meander through the divine tension of what I knew was right (to not have a body in pain and limitation) and what I was left living in (a fallible earthly body).

In my twenties, after being fully grown, I began having

surgeries to replace the worst of the joints. This provided me with some relief from pain as well as provided me with more freedom from physical limitations.

However, in my mid-twenties, the autoimmune disease attacked my spinal cord. After a misdiagnosis and being treated for the wrong condition for a couple of months, I became much worse in a very short period of time. Eventually, I became completely paralyzed from both shoulders down and had to be hospitalized. I no longer had any control over my bodily functions and had to rely on nurses and nurses' aids to keep me cleaned and changed. Other people had to feed, bathe, and dress me. I was completely helpless and had no say or control over what was going on in my body.

On top of that, I was a newlywed. We had been married for less than a year at this point and my husband and I were left to figure out how to traverse this enormous situation on our own. Things were pretty bleak for us and there were many voices of doom and gloom speaking death over our situation.

Extended family, full of meaning well, suggested that my husband could—perhaps even should—just quietly leave me. After all, we hadn't been married that long and who could blame him for leaving? The doctors said I would never walk again.

Part of the treatment given was chemotherapy and due to that, the doctors said I would never be able to conceive a child. The tension of life was swallowing us whole and for a while, we weren't sure what to believe or think. We didn't know who to turn to. But we knew that separating was not the answer. Praise God, my husband stuck things out with me.

It was a brutal process, but in spite of the doctor's pessimism, feeling slowly began to return to different parts of my body as the inflammation in my spinal cord began to disappear. It's a tricky business when nerves begin to wake up. Sometimes it feels like pins and needles and other times it feels like knives stabbing you or like your skin is on fire. But the feeling did return and slowly, but surely, I was able to start moving my body and walking again. After being in two different hospitals, and a nursing home, for a total of eight months, I was finally well enough to be released to go home with my husband.

Over time, a new strength began to come over me, not just in the physical sense but in a spiritual one as well. I can now look back and see that God never once left me. He was right there with me the whole time. In the middle of the pain, He was there. In the middle of the sorrow, He was there. In the middle of the questioning, He was there.

To this day I firmly believe that God has already healed me, however I am still waiting for that complete healing to manifest. In the meantime, I have learned how to not only survive the tension of life but to thrive within it. See, God had this amazing way of redeeming what the enemy caused for evil.

The struggles I endured have helped me see that the tension I lived in—the tension we all live in—can be used to draw us closer to our Abba Father. The divine discord between what we know is right, and what we are often faced with, causes us to be dependent on Him alone. He is not only the One with the answers but also the One with the solutions.

God is Lord over all of our days—good, bad and, well... ugly. But we don't have to wallow in the tension or pray that we merely survive it. We can thrive in the worst of days because He is with us, strengthening us all along the way.

Sometimes the greatest miracle isn't one of physical healing but one of peace, joy, and strength in the midst of a difficult time. And maybe, just maybe, if we stick it out long enough and trust our Abba with everything, then we will live to see a day when He will use us, and our darkest times, to help shine His Light to others.

> *"Blessed be the God and Father of our Lord Jesus Christ, the Father of mercies and God of all comfort, who comforts us in all our tribulation, that we may be able to comfort those who are in any trouble, with the comfort with which we ourselves are comforted by God."*
>
> ~ 2 Corinthians 1:3-4

Candid Conversation Starters

1) You may not be going through something as major as Karen was (or maybe you are), but do you ever feel overwhelmed by life? Do you let that tension keep you from focusing on God, or does it draw you closer to Him?

2) What thoughts or emotions are stirred up when you read Psalm 16?

3) Is there another way you related to what Karen shared in this chapter? If so, what was it?

Words Hurt

Sarah Coller

You have most likely heard the saying, "burn me once, shame on you; burn me twice, shame on me." I have never said that or believed it, but I think I am coming to sympathize with where it comes from.

Recently, someone hurt me badly, and probably permanently, with their words. Angry, accusing, and unfair words hurt—they kill. In fact, I think some words hurt more than actions. Especially written words, because you know they have been meditated over, read and reread, and then a conscious choice has been made to seal up that letter or to send that email.

> "Then Peter came and said to Him, 'Lord, how often shall my brother sin against me and I forgive him? Up to seven times?' Jesus said to him, 'I do not say to you, up to seven times, but up to seventy times seven.'"
>
> ~ Matthew 18:21-22, NASB

Jesus told us to forgive seventy times seven times. How

135

can this mesh with the "burn me" phrase above? There are two things I have learned to do with people who hurt me: speak truth and set boundaries.

Before I go on, let me be clear that I am not talking about the wishy-washy, fair-weather friend or the creep who cut you off at the Krispy Kreme, those kinds of conflicts are usually easily managed and don't stick to your bones too long. I'm talking about those you have a deeper, heart relationship with: long-time friends, parents, adult children, adult siblings, ex-spouses, etc.

3 Ways to Overcome Offenses

So, how do I handle situations where those I love have hurt me deeply? First, I speak truth. Conflict and negativity are unavoidable consequences of sin, but the best way to combat the enemy of our souls, who wants to keep us in that place of negativity, is to use words that are true.

1) Own Your Responsibility

Begin by owning your responsibility in the matter. Do what you can to offer resolution and ask for forgiveness where needed. So much of conflict resolution has to do with what is going on inside of you. You can't make someone forgive you, see your point of view, or change theirs. But you can make sure you have done everything God is requiring of you in the situation—mostly for your own peace and so you can move forward without regret.

2) Remember Your Freedom

Remember the things you have been forgiven for. Oftentimes, the conflict you are in now is the same conflict you have been in before. Is the person bringing up things from the past that you have already worked out and resolved? Is the person bringing up a sin you know God has already forgiven you for? You took that trash out long ago, don't let someone else bring it back in.

Remember the things you are not responsible for. You are not responsible for your parents' divorce, your sibling's failure, your adult child's finances, or your ex-spouse's relationships with others. You are not responsible for making someone else's life miserable. People choose to be miserable. Don't be one of them.

3) Set Boundaries

When you are speaking truth, either to the person or just to yourself, (you will need to speak it to yourself way more than you will to anyone else) you will find that you are able to think clearly enough to set proper boundaries. These will look different for each person and situation, and they will likely change over time as you heal and as your life changes.

Here are a few things to know about setting boundaries...

Setting boundaries is basically saying, here is a line we won't cross. It doesn't always have to be a negative thing. For instance, my brother and I disagree on many things. We both have similar moral codes, but we have different reactions to important issues. We love to discuss and debate for hours, but we have set up a boundary: we won't fight. We love each other too much to ever let those disagreements become personal.

Sometimes boundaries need to be set concerning time, influence, or even what topics can be discussed. Do what you can to maintain a peaceful relationship, so far as it depends on you (Romans 12:18). Learn to say, no.

Prepare for a change in your extended family dynamic or circle of friends by keeping a humble heart. Often, it's the people we are closest to that can be the most toxic in our own walk with God. Allowing angry, bitter, and hurting people to have a spiritual influence in our lives will not bring us closer to the Lord. We can love them from a distance, but we must be careful not to adopt a haughty attitude. Self-righteousness is not self-preservation.

Sometimes boundaries are going to be permanent. This is where both the "seventy times seven" and "burn me" phrases come into play. When I was a new wife and new Christian, one of the verses that always bugged me was Matthew 10:37 where Jesus tells us that anyone who loves his parents, children, etc. more than Him is not worthy of Him. The basic gist here is not that Christ is trying to separate us from the family we were born into, but that we need to count the cost of following Him.

We should be willing to forgive with reckless abandon. Holding onto offenses hurts you more than it hurts the other person. However, forgiveness doesn't always mean a happy reconciliation. Sometimes we do have to let go for good. How do you know if it's time? Talk to God about it. A lot. You will know it's right when He gives you unexplainable peace in your heart.

It is true that hurting people hurt others. I remember when I hurt someone I love with words that should have been left unsaid. My brother gave me some good advice a couple nights ago when he said we should always think about whether or not something needs to be said before saying it. Is it going to accomplish anything positive? Is it going to move you forward toward a closer relationship with this person and with Christ? If not, be careful to really think and pray it through before making a decision.

Let us be careful not to hurt one another with our words. And let it begin with me.

> *"Do not let any unwholesome talk*
> *come out of your mouths, but only what is helpful*
> *for building others up according to their needs,*
> *that it may benefit those who listen."*
> ~ Ephesians 4:29 (NIV)

Candid Conversation Starters

1) When you have been hurt by someone, what is your first instinct? Revenge, prayer, telling someone else, forgiveness, or something else?

2) God set boundaries known as the ten commandments. Take a moment to read over them (Exodus 20:1-21). Have you ever considered the commandments as boundaries before?

3) Do you struggle when it comes to setting your own boundaries? How does that affect your life?

4) Is there another way you related to what Sarah shared in this chapter? If so, what was it?

Singing Through The Spirit

Stacey Louiso

*"I thank God, whom I serve with a pure conscience ...
as without ceasing I remember you in my prayers night
and day, greatly desiring to see you, being mindful of
your tears, that I may be filled with joy, when I call to
remembrance the genuine faith that is in you ...
Therefore I remind you to stir up the gift of God which
is in you through the laying on of my hands. For God
has not given us a spirit of fear, but of power and of
love and of a sound mind."*

~ 2 Timothy 1:3-7 (NKJV)

The day after I had moved my belongings out of the home of my marriage was a Sunday, and I was supposed to be off from singing in the Praise Band at church. But, as it happened, both the worship leader and our other singer had a gig, so they weren't going to be there. Mind you, I had asked for this time off over a month in advance and provided a short explanation why to the director. He approached me a week or two before that day asking if I could please sing since they would both be absent.

I was a bit upset and a lot disappointed, but I agreed to do it; I honestly didn't know how I would have it in me to get up in front of everyone, including my spouse who ran the soundboard.

The night before, being overly emotional and exhausted from moving, I pulled out my Bible and cried out to my Lord to guide me through His Word and give me strength I didn't have on my own. Ending up in a puddle of tears while on my face in prayer, I beseeched Him to take me away and replace me with a singing angel the next morning. I'd had to make a similar request, for Him to completely take over my voice on many a Sunday morning since I joined the Praise Band, due to lack of sleep or being upset and empty over the previous months.

My Lord lifted me up from that place on the floor, while showering me with His agape love, and helped me drift off to sleep. The next morning, I was exhausted, but as God's Word promises, *"...there may be weeping in the night, but joy comes in the morning"* (Psalm 30:5, NKJV).

I was filled with His joy, life, and vigor. A weight had been lifted and I was fueled, ready to worship and praise my Lord. During our time of rehearsal prior to service, the sound guy disappeared. I discovered the microphone was not picking up my voice as it normally did, and it was preventing the band from hearing me and causing issues. He didn't fix it once we started either!

I wonder how it must have been, to see the wife who had moved out just the night before, up on stage singing her heart out for God—joyfully! I know how it felt for me: liberating.

But, honestly, it was not "me" up there, it was my body filled with the Holy Spirit; exactly as I prayed God would do for this servant. At one point, I could sense the band getting frustrated that they still weren't hearing me and I felt myself grab the mic off the stand, nearly jamming it in my mouth. As I did this, I kid you not, a fire ignited within. The enemy was not winning that morning because my God is greater than he who is living in the world!

This singular incident had such an impact on my healing. I knew I was going to be okay as I walked through and out the other end of this trial; but what God did that morning was show me not only His glory, but His power. He showed up in that room and took control.

God reminded me of the verse from 2 Timothy 1:7, *"For God has not given us a spirit of fear, but of power and of love and of a sound mind"* (NKJV). You see, before God took back my voice for His use, anything happening in my personal life would have overcome me. I would have trembled on stage with anxiety and crumbled into tears. Can I please express to you what an amazing gift this is to me, and a tribute to God, that this no longer occurs? It is amazing to compare the woman who tried to control this life (me) to the God who does control it, if we allow Him the honor.

Psalm 30 truly exemplifies how I feel when I have absolutely nothing of myself to give, yet simply by asking, He fills me up and uses me despite where I am emotionally, physically or mentally: *"I will extol thee, O Lord; for thou hast lifted me up, and hast not made my foes to rejoice over me. O Lord my God, I cried unto thee, and thou hast healed me. O Lord, thou hast brought up my soul from the grave: thou hast kept me alive, that I should not go down to the pit. Sing unto the Lord, O ye saints of his, and give thanks at the remembrance of his holiness...To the end that my glory may sing praise to thee, and not be silent. O Lord my God, I will give thanks unto thee for ever"* (verses 1-4, 12, KJV).

Thank You, Lord Jesus, for overcoming that which could have debilitated me. For showing up when I needed You most and showing Your glory in those moments, as not to claim it for myself. I praise You, Jesus, the Savior of this broken world and my broken heart, for making me whole and filling so many holes. There is *none* like You, Jesus! Amen.

Candid Conversation Starters

1) Do you trust God to be your strength when you are weak, or is this an area you struggle in? Can you remember a time when He gave you supernatural strength to get though a situation?

2) How can the truth found in Romans 8:38-39 help you when your heart is hurting? Take a moment to read Isaiah 55.

3) Is there another way you related to what Stacey shared in this chapter? If so, what was it?

The Grace of God

Debbie Erickson

My whole world went black. Fear gripped me like never before as it wrapped its tentacles around me. Something was happening, but I didn't know what. I felt as though I was doomed, and I knew no one could help me. No one... Except God.

It was then that I did what any Christian would probably do in a situation like this: I fell prostrate on the floor and cried out to God. I felt empty, alone, and helpless. It was just me and God. I had been forced to come to God's throne... alone.

When I have since looked back at that time, I realize it couldn't have been any other way. I believe God had put me in a position where there was no one to look to who could have helped me but Him. When you read my story, I believe you will understand why...

I had attended a somewhat legalistic congregation after I first gave my life to the Lord, but I believe that my brothers and sisters in Christ only wanted to serve God and put Him first in all things. And so did I.

I grew in the Lord while enduring some of life's

hardships (struggling with deep depression twice was the worst). Even though I was around other Christians, I always felt as if I was walking alone and that there was really no one who could truly understand my problems, or who had experienced the same things I was experiencing. So, I would mostly keep things to myself because I really had no hope of anyone who could help me.

Life went on. I would read my Bible before going to bed because I wanted His Word to be the last thing in my mind. I had a close relationship with God and prayed fervently for my unborn daughters—that they would grow up and give their lives to Christ, and that they would marry Christian men. (Praise Him for answering those prayers.) With God's help, I overcame the depression, which wasn't an easy road, but I continued my walk with the Lord with a sincere and fervent heart.

I have read many verses concerning God's grace, and I have also read many books on the subject over the years. Sadly, after reading the last book on grace, I set the book down and said, "I just don't get it." I didn't get God's grace. It sounded too good to be true, which is how many have felt. How could He forgive me for this, or for that? I, like many others before me, felt like God's finger was always pointing at me asking, "How could you?" And, like a child who gets reprimanded, I would drop my head, hunch my shoulders in disgrace, and think *how despicable.*

After years of "not getting it", the day came when God so graciously and mercifully helped me "get it." He had to help me understand His grace because of His love for me. It was like He said, "All right, enough is enough. It's time you understand My grace."

One night, a deep, deep feeling of despair washed over

me. I was placed into submission before God; a place where I felt no one could help me but Him, and Him alone. I cried to God and remember thinking, *It's just me and You, God. No one can come to my rescue except You. No one can save me from myself except You alone.*

God alone. There I was, at the foot of God's throne, just Him and me. And I was scared. A shaky scared. I realized that He was the only One who could save me from myself. And I also believe it was the only way He could get through to me.

As though a flood-gate had opened, He spoke to my heart silently and tenderly. His words rushed through me, *"My grace is sufficient for thee: My strength is made perfect in weakness..."* (2 Corinthians 12:9, KJV). I had read this verse many times, and sadly, I had always felt like it was a verse for everyone but me. Sadder still, I had lived the majority of my Christian life thinking this.

Where was the joy? There was none. How could there be? When all you feel is fear, how can you ever experience God's joy? Or faith? I didn't have the faith to believe that this verse was for me too, so I lived in fear of God and it was unhealthy.

But God reached down to me that night because of His love for me. And I was in a position to accept His love, forgiveness, and mercy. He cared enough to open my eyes to something that I couldn't see or understand for myself through the years. I believe He had to turn off the lights in my world in order to bring me to the footstool of His grace and help me truly understand that *"His grace is sufficient for me"* too. My greatest regret was that it took me so long to get it. Evidently, no one had been successful in helping me understand it along the way.

I hope, by this short testimony, that if you don't get God's grace, you will be able to. God's grace is sufficient for you, too, because love covers a multitude of sins. I implore you, don't go one more second not realizing the extent of God's grace even if it means you waking up each morning saying and claiming 2 Corinthians 12:9.

In the end, it is just you and God. He loves us so much and that love is the reason His grace is sufficient. God's grace isn't a license for us to sin, but His grace covers us when we slip up and do. God showed up for me, and when I rose from the ashes of my fears, I had a better understanding of His grace. And He can do that for you as well.

Candid Conversation Starters

1) Do you "get" God's grace? How would you describe it, or how do you struggle when it comes to understanding it?

2) Read Ephesians 2:8-9 and Hebrews 4:16 and explore why understanding God's grace is important.

3) Is there another way you related to what Debbie shared in this chapter? If so, what was it?

The Motives of My Heart

Sylvia Brown-Roberts

"Kat, always remember the Lord. Make time to worship Him on the first day of the week. He never forgets you. He blesses you each day."

My daughter gives me the look. Translation: "I know. You tell me that every week, Mom, but you know that I am out of town on the weekends. That's the only time I have to hang out with my friends."

This is the frequent interaction between my 22-year-old college graduate daughter and myself about her waning church attendance. She was raised in the church, baptized at the age of 12, and she gleefully attended worship services. She imitated me in singing hymns and developed a sweet soprano voice. Once she was baptized, she eagerly took communion every Sunday. She seemed to enjoy church services and activities. Her father and I were so pleased that she loved the Lord.

However, things shifted when she went to college. She lived on campus but was close enough that we could pick her up on Sunday, so she could participate in worship services. Eventually, her father and I noticed that she seemed less interested in the whole church thing, but she did attend and join us for family dinner after we left church.

Like many of today's college graduates, she had a challenge finding work in her desired career. This was a disappointment for her. She moved back home with us so she could work at other jobs while she looked for the desired one. That way, she could save money, start repayment of her student loans, and move into her own place. As always, she had our support. We encouraged her to be strong and stay close to the Lord. I reminded her that God still blesses us even when everything doesn't fall into place the way we want.

> *"And let us consider one another to provoke unto love and good works; Not forsaking the assembling of ourselves together as the manner of some is; but exhorting one another and so much the more, as ye see the day approaching."*
> ~ Hebrews 10:24-25 (KJV)

At first, she worked all week and went away for the weekend to hang out with friends, but she always returned home in time for worship on Sundays. Then, she worked all week, went away for the weekend, and came home on Monday morning in time to get dressed for work. Later, she went straight to work on Monday without coming home to get dressed. I guess she got dressed for work at the home of her friends and then went to work. To her credit, she always called to inform us she wasn't coming back on Sunday night because she didn't want us to worry about her safety.

I tried to remember that she was no longer a teenager and

that she was respectful to her parents, but it began to bother me that she was "forsaking the assembly."

I developed an attitude about this. I repeatedly reminded and cautioned her about making time for work and friends but being too busy for God. I prayed for her. Then I prayed about the way I was handling this situation, and God blessed me to examine myself, to check my motives.

Was I being self-righteous? Did I want Kat to attend worship for *me*? Was I more concerned about appearances at church? Was I trying to use parental control to make 22-year-old Kat attend worship? Did I want to win a battle of the wills with her? Was I more interested in being right than I was about her soul? Was I showing my daughter a Christ-like spirit?

God gave me a clear moment. I remembered Proverbs 3:5-6: *"Trust in the Lord with all thine heart; and lean not on thine own understanding. In all thy ways acknowledge him and he shall direct thy paths"* (KJV).

Weeks have passed, and God has settled my spirit about having the right attitude while I am doing the right thing. Today is Friday, and I kid you not, when I returned home from the gym this afternoon, Kat approached me, smiled, and volunteered her weekend plans to me. "Mom, I will be traveling on Saturday, but I will be home in time for church on Sunday."

I replied, "That's music to my ears, Kat." In my mind, I prayed, *Thank you, Heavenly Father.*

Candid Conversation Starters

1) Can you think of a time when you wanted the right thing for the wrong reason?

2) Do you ever evaluate your own faith by the performance of your children? Or do you ever allow something other than your faith in Christ to determine your standing as a Christian? Read Romans 3:23-25 and 8:38-39.

3) Is there another way you related to what Sylvia shared in this chapter? If so, what was it?

Bitter Prayers
Heather Hart

"Pray for us?" She asked so expectantly, detailing a little bit of what was going on in her family. My friend needed prayer, and she asked me because she knew I would. She was right, but I still felt a little bit miffed. This was the third person in just as many days who had done this.

Didn't they understand that my head hurt? Did they not know what was going on in my own life? Yes, God gave me a heart for others, and yes, I believe in the power of prayer, but if you looked around, you would have noticed that my prayers didn't seem to be very effective as of late.

My husband needed back surgery and we got the runaround and ultimately denial by workers comp. The injury happened in October, it was now January and the surgery still hadn't come to pass. I had been experiencing debilitating migraines for over six months and we still didn't have any answers.

We were in pain, stressed beyond measure, and clinging to Jesus for dear life, but sure, I'd pray for her while I was there. Sadly, that was my sarcasm-filled attitude that morning before I lifted up my friend in prayer. It wasn't that I didn't love my friend, I do. And quite frankly there is no excuse for my sinful attitude, but my head hurt, I was cranky, and in all my humanness it came out in all its ugliness... Just as it had on the two other unsuspecting Christian sisters who had asked for prayer earlier that weekend who never even knew how bitter I was.

My attitude was sinfully wrong. I have humbled myself before God and repented of my sin. And because I do love my friend and I do believe in the power of prayer, I went ahead and began to pray for her request: A humble prayer, bringing her words before Jesus. But God didn't leave it there. Prayer just happens to be a two-way street.

What started out as a meek, half-hearted, obligatory prayer, became so much more. The more I prayed, the more passionate I became. God moved in my heart, first for my friend, then for myself. He broke my heart for her, and then for how bitter I was about her request.

It was so unlike me, unlike anything I had ever been, that it caught me off guard. How long had I been letting my pain push out the love of Jesus?

When I finished praying, everything was still the same as before. My head still hurt, my husband still needed surgery, our bills were still piling up, but God had changed my heart. I felt renewed and refreshed in a way I hadn't for weeks. Even though I had been clinging to Jesus there was something about truly pouring my heart out for someone else that refilled me like nothing else had.

Have you ever been there? Have you ever found life leaving you bitter? Your situation might not have anything to do with health issues, prayer, or finances, but I think we can all lose sight of what's really important from time to time.

I am reminded of a biblical account from the Old Testament. The Israelites were in the wilderness of Zin complaining about not having water. They were just sure they were going to die, and they were probably pretty bitter about their situation.

Thus, Moses and Aaron went into the tent of meeting to pray on their behalf. God instructed Moses to tell a rock to yield its water, but Moses threw a little fit. Instead of doing as God instructed, he turned to the people, chastised them, and then beat the rock. It would probably be safe to say he was a bit bitter himself.

Bitterness gets the best of all of us from time to time. It's what we do when we realize we are bitter that matters. We serve a forgiving God. He doesn't keep a running tally of our failures because we have all sinned and fallen short of the glory of God (Romans 3:23). One sin is all it takes to separate us from Him, so He doesn't need a tally. All He needs to know is if we are covered by the blood of Christ.

God doesn't want us to live life with a bitter heart, He wants us to be full of joy. But in order to do that, we have to be willing to let Him work in our hearts. Just like He did for me that day.

Oh, and for the record, God did answer my prayers for my friend. He gave her just what we asked for in prayer. I know that sometimes His answer is no, but sometimes His answer is yes, and I needed that reminder.

Candid Conversation Starters

1) Can you think of a specific time you realized you had become bitter about something? What was it?

2) Bitter is the opposite of content. How can bitterness affect our faith? (See Hebrews 12:14-15)

3) Is there another way you related to what Heather shared in this chapter? If so, what was it?

Finding My Place

Laura J. Marshall

Make me small, God, smaller still. Cover me under Your wings. Let me weep at Your feet and lament the ills of men.

I have heard the stories, been part of one; assaulted and discarded. The woman who related her experience of escaping with her life was poised, beautiful, accomplished. Yet tears shown in her eyes. After meeting, talking, connecting, and parting, I came home and wanted to curl into a ball and cry.

Not that she isn't the victor, she is. Yet, I feel somehow the need to mark this moment in time. Feel the Holy Spirit's call to hush, reverence. The touch of the divine in saving, in being, and still existing.

And I wonder at my role in this brush with this woman. I feel the need to elevate and help her in her endeavors to get her story out and her ministry. Yet that selfish voice whispers, *"Where do I fit in here, Father?"*

I feel Your call to be the foot washer, the one who holds the robe, carries the towel, disappears in the crowd so Jesus can be lifted higher and be seen.

I remember the Scripture about the least (Luke 9:48); however, having it come to mind taints me. The pride of my humanity and who You created me to be rises up. I want to push myself to the front and hear the prophesy over *me*, though it's never come forth.

To remain hidden is greater. Is it that I am to pave the way for another, as John the Baptist did for Jesus? How do we balance pride and service? Can I point to another and help shine the light there? Is it in my mediocrity, my quiet desire to be alone with You that You will thrust me forward? And why do I desire that in the deep places of my heart?

To be hidden is... safety. I want to remain *safe*, yet is there more glory for You in the high places?

You know my heart, God. The secret prideful places, the scared lonely places, the brokenness in not knowing, not doing, serving to serve and not to be the *Whosoever* in the least among us, but *truly* be the least and in Your eyes only, the greatest.

I am broken again. Perhaps this is Your will.

How do we know whether to push for greatness or sweep, wash, toil, and prepare for the one that has Your call on their life?

The Bible says that You are the God who sees me (Genesis 16:13). In this fast-paced digital world, with camera phones capturing every moment of our existence, I see a trend. Everyone is looking for someone to *see* them.

It is my great pleasure to be reminded that You are the God who sees me. Never will I be alone or forgotten. Whether I am in a season of being left to myself, one among a crowd, or the center of attention, You are the One who sees me.

It has been a day and distance has helped me ache less for the woman I met, yet compassion stirs. I have finished my regular work-day, made dinner, talked to my children, and sat with my dog. And I see inside me all that every human has desired who walks the earth. They want to be seen, heard, comforted, and lifted up. You do all of these things for me... for all of us, God.

Whether I am the least, the greatest, in pain, or at the pinnacle of accomplishment, it's freeing to know You see. Bend down Your ear to hear me, for every once in a while I ask, *make me small, God, smaller still. Cover me under Your wings. Let me weep at Your feet and lament the ills of men.*

Candid Conversation Starters

1) Do you ever feel like you are completely alone, or like no one understands what you are going through? If so, share about the last time you felt that way.

2) Read Luke 9:46-48. Do you focus more on your own success or on sharing the love of Jesus with those you come in contact with?

3) How do you handle encounters with other women? Are you more likely to pray for them or judge them?

4) Is there another way you related to what Laura shared in this chapter? If so, what was it?

Writing The Next Chapter

Baby Jeudy Dorzion

All looked dimmed as I walked down the narrow path to purchase my mother's cigarettes. I had no other route to take besides the one that I feared the most. Although I lived in a highly dangerous country, I didn't fear my environment but who I would encounter on the way to my destination.

It took years of self-doubt, loss of identity, and self-affliction for me to finally pinpoint where I was served a spoonful of hopelessness for the first time. 20 years later, many sleepless nights and many questions "why" to God was what it took for me to accept and acknowledge that I had a problem that wasn't just skin deep—its roots ran all the way down to my core.

In my late teen years, I found myself emotionally in pain, mentally lost and confused, and physically uncomfortable. Like many teens, I blamed my mother for it all. My situation was very different though because my mother was killed when I was eight years old.

From a very young age, as long as I could remember, I cannot say I had a connection with my mother. I remember her being mean and mad most of the time. I remember her smoking cigarettes and I had to go buy them for her. I remember she wasn't there to protect me when, on my way to get her cigarettes, I was molested by the next-door neighbors.

I don't remember loving her. I don't remember much about my mother; that is why I am on this journey of giving birth to myself. It's because I want to believe we shared laughter, goodnight kisses, hugs, and daily talks.

Through my studies of psychology, counseling, and human behavior, I have learned that when we suffer a loss or trauma our hearts can literally feel like they have been shattered into a million pieces. Or we may feel like our heart has broken open and we are bleeding metaphorically. At times, it can even be difficult to breathe because we surround ourselves with the guilt of many questions.

6 Steps Toward Healing A Broken Heart

It is time for healing. No more covering it up. No more hiding. It is understandable, but the longer we avoid our pain and attempt to push it away, the more difficult it is to break out of the paralysis. Trust me I know, it took me 17 years to acknowledge that I had a problem and five more years after that to accept help from family, friends, and professionals.

That was a very hard time in my life. Not knowing the warmth of my mother's love plus the regular feminine hormones kicked things up a notch. I can proudly say today that I honestly went through some very dark times dealing with depression. I took the following steps to heal my brokenness.

Step 1: Struggling With Denial

Denial is the first round of defense that we immediately enter into, like the first chamber in the heart that breaks. In this inner chamber we face the demons trying every which way to not accept our reality. It's as if a visitor with bad news has entered our home, and we try to push him/her back outside so we don't have to face the painful image of the woman in the mirror.

Step 2: Acknowledging Our Brokenness

We must begin to acknowledge to ourselves that something is wrong. Step into the experience of attempting to tolerate the unbearable quality of this truth that our normal is abnormal. I say "attempt" to deal with the brokenness, as we have to acknowledge the truth so over time we can learn to manage, handle, and heal it.

Step 3: Surrender

The song "I Surrender" by Hillsong reminds me of the many times I have had to surrender to God asking Him to take control of my life and save me. So many times, I was close to giving up but, glory be to God, He never left my side.

My friends remember that the step of entering into the chamber of surrender is an essential stage in order to allow oneself to begin the strenuous process of mending a broken heart and healing from depression. When we surrender, we enter the state of not knowing and not doing. Since we do not know just how long the journey will take, allow God to have His way in you.

Step 4: Acceptance

It takes great courage to pull yourself up off the floor, bed, or couch and get back into the world when all you see is sadness within and around you. Acceptance gives us the first few steps we need to begin to slowly scratch and claw our way back into the land of the living. Join a church, and other positive local groups that will help you be around positive people and activities. We must get out and get active.

Step 5: Embrace the Now

We tend to live in the past, reliving the trauma or memories of the one or things we have lost. Now, memories are important to maintain, but within reason. In order to take the next step, we must embrace the present to manifest the future.

One of the easiest and most effective techniques that I recommend to everyone is reading the Bible. What does God says about our future? What promises does He have for us? What do we have to look forward to? It can be hard to let go of the pain and eventually release and transform it into vitality, acceptance and equanimity. Other methods to help one become more present include: exercising, long drives, walks in nature, or visiting museums.

Step 6: Giving Birth to Our Future

Matthew 6:31-33 says, *"Therefore do not be anxious, saying, 'What shall we eat?' or 'What shall we drink?' or 'What shall we wear?' For the Gentiles seek after all these things, and your heavenly Father knows that you need them all. But seek first the kingdom of God and his righteousness, and all these things will be added to you."*

There is a field of thinking within positive psychology that says the way through pain includes becoming your own architect and actively engaging and involving yourself in the planning of a new future. The victim in us will want to remain on the floor curled up in agony, wishing to avoid any future painful experiences that life may present to us. One who is engaged and empowered realizes and accepts that the past is the past and all we have now is the present moment and the future.

It is all in the next breath in and the next breath out and creating in our mind's eye a future storyline for ourselves. Dare to dream and be wild with your imagination. Have the courage to dream any positive, loving, creative future with no bounds. Remember, after death comes rebirth!

It's your storyline you are creating, like writing the next chapter of your life in a novel. Nevertheless, in your story I challenge you to *jump* into the water, catch the next wave and maybe you will be surprised and delighted to experience yourself riding that new wave with confidence, joy, and possibility. Give birth to your blessings!

Candid Conversation Starters

1) Is something that happened to you as a child holding you back from living an abundant life? If so, what is it?

2) Read 2 Corinthians 5:17. What does that mean to you?

3) Is there another way you related to what Baby Jeudy shared in this chapter? If so, what was it?

Time To Get Candid

Heather Hart

Could you relate to any of the stories in this book? While I couldn't relate to all of them, it would be fair to say I could relate to many of them in one way or another. That's because these stories were written by women just like me; by women just like you.

These stories were written by women who love Jesus, but who also live in the real world. If that defines you too, I encourage you to join in and start having your own candid conversations. You can start by being candid with God about the way you are feeling, about what is going on in your life. Then, start opening up to the women God has placed in your life. Come alongside a Christian sister who is struggling and let her know she is not alone.

While I couldn't relate to all the stories in this book, and we can't always relate to everything someone else is going through, we can always remember that God loves them. We can listen to their stories and try to love them without judging them. We can treat them the way we want to be treated (Luke 6:31); we can treat them the way Jesus would treat them.

So how do we have a candid conversation?

I am an introvert by nature, so random conversations are hard for me. But part of having candid conversations is making them a piece of who we are. We don't have to go out of our way every time, but simply learn to open up.

For me, this started with my Bible study group. I went every week and got comfortable enough with that group of women that I started feeling like I could be honest with them. For you, it may be inviting someone out for coffee or mentoring someone. It may even start in your own home with your own children or at work with a coworker. Candid conversations work best when they aren't a one-time thing— a forced conversation—but part of a relationship. That's the beauty of them.

Candid conversations become part of who we are and minister to everyone we come in contact with. They happen when we look beyond the exterior and start asking questions. Not just a simple, "how are you?" but digging deeper, showing listeners that we actually want to know the real answer and have the time to listen. That is why relationships are important. And God created us for relationships. We were never meant to go through life on our own.

I graduated high school a year early, and there was a time when all my friends were still in school, then they all went off to college. I had decided to wait to get my degree and was already married with my first child. My husband cheated on me, and eventually filed for divorce. I felt as if there wasn't a single person I could really talk to. I felt alone. It brought a whole new meaning to the phrase "all I have is Christ".

I would lay awake at night and beg God to bring a Christian friend into my life. I wanted God to be enough, but I also craved connection. The people at my church tried to make me feel welcome, but no one really reached out, not truly. They smiled at me and greeted me at church, but during the week I was alone.

I tried to get involved in Bible study, but they called to confirm I was indeed interested in coming enough times that I felt like they didn't want me there. They weren't calling to see how I was, but they didn't want to waste money on a book if I wasn't going to make it. I so wanted to be part of that study group. I wanted to have Christian friends; any friends… But I backed out because I didn't feel welcome.

Those Christians will never know how much hurt they caused me, but that is not why I am sharing this with you. I am sharing it because none of us were candid. I didn't tell them how much I wanted to attend. I just kept saying, "Yes, I'm planning to be there and looking forward to it." I could have avoided the whole ordeal if I just would have sat down with one of them and opened up. But I didn't. They saw me as a 19-year-old, college dropout, and single mom. Other than graduating high school early, I am sure it looked like I was a complete flake.

That is why candid conversations matter. They can help bridge gaps and guard against misunderstandings. They can help strengthen relationships. But ultimately, they should point to Jesus: Because each of our struggles, and all of our trials and temptations were covered with the blood of Christ. That's the gospel. Jesus didn't die just so we could get into Heaven, He came so that we could have a relationship with Him and a full life (John 10:10).

Candid conversations help us to live life abundantly and help us help others do the same. They refuse to give Satan a foothold. When we get candid, we dismantle the lie that we are in this alone; the lie that no one else understands what we are going through.

Candid conversations remind us that Jesus is the solution, no matter what our problem is.

Where To Go From Here

I pray that you read something in this book you can relate to; something that pointed you to Jesus, and let you know that you aren't in this life alone. But I also hope you take what you have read here and carry it with you. I pray you are inspired to start your own candid conversations with those you come in contact with. That you would let others know they don't have to walk alone.

When I first began opening up to others and having candid conversations, there were two Bible verses that helped me more than anything else. A short prayer based on Acts 4:29, *Lord, enable me to speak Your Word with great boldness.* And a reminder found in 1 Thessalonians 5:24: *"The one who calls you is faithful, and he will do it"* (NIV).

If you want to begin having your own candid conversations, prayer is a great place to start. Pray for God to soften your heart to the people around you and give you the strength to candidly share your own struggles in a way that points to Christ.

We all need Jesus, so let's get candid about it.

Like This Book?

❖ Join the movement by sharing your struggles and using them to point to Jesus—be sure to tag them with #CandidlyChristian on social media.

❖ Visit our website, CandidlyChristian.com, where real women get candid about their life and faith every week.

❖ Join our Candid Conversations Facebook group at: Facebook.com/groups/CandidConversations

❖ Review *Candid Conversations* on Amazon, your blog, and/or another online retailer.

❖ Tell your friends and family about this book.

About Heather Hart

Heather Hart is an internationally best-selling and award-winning author with an unquenchable passion for Jesus. She knows one thing every girl needs is a little honesty, so she's not afraid to get candid and share her struggles. Her hope is that through her writing, she can help others soak up the love of Jesus.

Heather currently resides in a small Texas town with her husband, Paul, and their four quickly-growing children. You can connect with her online by visiting her website BooksFaithandCoffee.com.

Contributing Authors

Sylvia Brown-Roberts

Sylvia Brown-Roberts is the author of three Christian Fiction novels. Her "Church Doors" series titles are: Behind Church Doors, Beyond Church Doors, and Behind and Beyond Church Doors: Promises. Nikolis McQuaige, the main character in the novels, is a single woman who attempts to walk in faith regardless of life's challenges. These challenges include interactions with the lively characters in and out of the church.

Sylvia is a retired public school teacher who has been actively involved with a congregation for many years. She has presented her novels at conferences, churches, workshops, and at bookstores. You can visit Sylvia online on her website SylviaBrownRoberts.com.

Stephanie M. Carter

Stephanie M. Carter is an author, speaker, minister and life coach of Grace to Live Coaching as well as a certified forgiveness coach with Forgiving Forward ministries. She is the mom of two sons. She is a passionate lover of Jesus Christ. She has her Doctorate in Theology and resides in the Atlanta, Georgia area. Her purpose in life is to instill discipline, integrity, and uncompromising spirit within women in their lives. You can visit Stephanie online at StephanieMCarter.com.

Sherry Chamblee

Sherry Chamblee is an aspiring author of Christian fiction, mom of six, wife to a cool dude, and caregiver to his granny. She is doing her best to let God do His best in her, and often failing, but trying to get back up again. You can connect with her online at SherryChamblee.weebly.com

Sarah Coller

Sarah Coller is the author of, *Now: Living Life to the Full, Right Where You Are*; as well as the popular blogs Classical Homemaking and Belle's Library. She lives in Northwest Arkansas with her husband of 18 years and her nine children. You can find Sarah online at ClassicalHomemaking.com.

Joi Copeland

Joi Copeland is married to a wonderful man, Chris, and has three amazing boys, Garrison, Gage, and Gavin. She lives in Denver, Colorado, but within the year, hopes to be living in Galway, Ireland. Joi's love of writing began at a young age. She wrote short stories for several years, and in 2009, she began writing her first novel, *Hope for Tomorrow*. You can learn more about Joi by visiting her online at JoiCopeland.com.

Baby Jeudy Dorzion

Baby Jeudy Dorzion, AKA "Coach Baby", was born in Haiti

and became a homeless orphan at a young age. Yet no matter what she faced God was always there for her and it is by His grace that she is here today.

Coach Baby is on a mission to share her testimony about how God can take a nobody and turn them into a successful business owner, mother, and wife. With her eloquent yet transparent approach she is committed to empowering women who are at the edge ready to jump into their calling. She currently resides in Alaska, where she is a proud member of the Christian Worship Center and serves in the Homeless Women's ministry. She is also a thriving business owner, life and business coach. Find out more by visiting her online at GivingBirthToAQueen.com.

Cristine Eastin

Cristine Eastin writes contemporary women's fiction spiced with romance, threaded with life's heartaches, and enriched with faith and hope. Cris grew up in Minnesota where life centered on family and friends, outdoor activities, pets, music, and reading. She also wrote short stories and terrible poetry. Then the fun writing stopped and she attended the university. She earned a doctorate in counseling from the University of Wisconsin-Madison. A psychotherapist for over thirty years, Cris has a passion for encouraging people.

Writing for fun again, Cris hopes her fiction not only entertains but pours into readers' deepest needs. She and her husband live in Wisconsin, not too far from the grandkids. Visit Cris at her website, CristineEastin.com, and take a peek at her novels *Fifty Days to Sunrise* and *Love Inherited*.

Janet Perez Eckles

Although blind, Janet Perez Eckles has been inspiring thousands to see the best in life. Her journey from trials to triumph appear in more than 28 anthologies, and in her own releases, including #1 bestselling *Simply Salsa: Dancing without Fear at God's Fiesta*. You can learn more about Janet and connect with her online at JanetPerezEckles.com.

Debbie Erickson

Debbie's love of writing began at an early age. She enjoys encouraging and inspiring others through her writing, and to discover their God-given purpose so they can grow their faith and passion and pay it forward to spread the love of Christ. God and Jesus Christ are the Rocks of her salvation and the air beneath her wings, and partners in her life's journey.

Beyond writing, she enjoys family times, her dog Ringo, and spending time with her husband who is the love of her life. He taught her how to golf twenty years ago, and they've been golfing ever since. Debbie also enjoys spending time outdoors in the summer working in the yard and gardening. You can connect with her online at Debra-Erickson.com.

Mary C. Findley

Mary C. Findley has poured her real life into her writing. From the cover designs inspired by her lifelong art studies to the love of pets and country life that worm their way into her historicals. The never-say-die heroes in her twenty-some fiction works are inspired by her husband, a crazy smart man with whom she co-writes science and history-based nonfiction. She's a strong believer in helping others and also has books about publishing and the need to have strong standards in reading and writing.

You can find Mary online at ElkJerkyForTheSoul.com.

Jaime Hampton

Jaime Hampton lives in Southcentral Alaska with her husband and three children. She has been involved in ministry with children and youth for over twenty years. Jaime writes Christian nonfiction and has a passion for studying the Bible. She also enjoys camping with her family, roasting (and drinking!) coffee, and the crazy life that comes with being a hockey mom. You can connect with Jaime at JaimeHampton.com.

Rebecca Hastings

Rebecca believes in embracing grace in real life. At My Ink Dance, she captures hard, uncomfortable, often unspoken feelings and brings light, honesty and God's truth to them in a relatable way. She is also the author of Worthy: Believe Who God Says You Are, a 20-day devotional inviting women to live life confident of their worth. Rebecca is a wife and mother of three in Connecticut writing imperfect and finding faith along the way.

Beth Kelly

Beth Kelly has had a love of writing ever since she was small and enjoys writing in various styles and on a variety of topics.

She is passionate about using her writing to reach others for Christ and has recently started a growing ministry for women Standing for their Marriages.

Beth has a background in Occupational Therapy in which she has worked in a variety of settings and continues to work on-call. She recently became a Certified Biblical Life Coach and a Certified Marriage Breakthrough Coach. She resides in Minnesota with her husband and two young children and enjoys gardening (especially creating fairy gardens with her daughter), exploring new places, and reading Christian Fiction. You can visit Beth's online home, Blogging For Her, at MyInnerRapunzel.com.

Lynn Landes

Lynn Landes is the author and independent publisher of multiple books in all age brackets. Her stories span the spectrum of Romantic Fiction from historical, paranormal, romantic suspense to Christian fantasy including the best-selling Covenant Series. You can find the first book in that series on Amazon at amazon.com/dp/B00FA1MZA2.

Cheryl Long

Cheryl is a disciple of Jesus Christ since 1997 and is married to Terry. She has been practicing the art of mothering for 34 years and three boys and eight girls call her "Mom," She is also "grandma" to 5 precious ones, thus far.

Her passions include learning to be the wife God created her to be, homeschooling and discipling her children, creating "scrapbook videos," and writing and ministering to women through various avenues. She shares life lessons on her Facebook page The Long Way to Go.

Stacey Louiso

A disciple of Jesus Christ and adventurer in spirit, Stacey Louiso aspires to make the world a better, more positive place. She attributes any successes to her personal relationship with Jesus Christ who gives her hope and strength through all things. Stacey was co-author and editor of the Christian non-fiction book *Walking Through Fiery Trials: A Year of Loss, Learning and Faith* with the wonderful Mary Pat Jones. In 2018, her testimonial memoir, *Bound by Seduction, Redeemed by Grace: One Woman's Story of Falling into Freedom (Xulon Press)*, will be released. You can find out more about her at WritingDownLife.com

Laura J. Marshall

Laura J. Marshall works a full-time job, runs several small businesses, is an author, and has been raising five sons for almost a quarter of a century. She is a best-selling author of shorter length books in various Christian genres: historical and contemporary romance, Amish, suspense, children's, young adult, and nonfiction.

Visit her on her website to connect at LauraJMarshall.com

Sheila Qualls

Sheila Qualls gives women tools to minimize the effects of emotional baggage in marriage.

Through a window of humor and transparency, she shares her successes and failures to encourage wives in nurturing and strengthening their marriages. You can follow her on Facebook at The Not So Excellent Wife or on her blog at SheilaQualls.com. You can also find her on the MOPS Blog, Scary Mommy, Grown and Flown, The Mighty, and Crosswalk.com.

Laura Rath

Laura Rath enjoys writing to encourage women in their walk with Christ. She shares stories of her own faith journey on her blog, Journey in Faith (LauraRath.blogspot.com), and is a regular contributor for several Christian websites, including Candidly Christian, LifeLetter Café, and Thoughts About God. Laura is a wife and mother and enjoys spending time with her family, reading, going deeply into God's Word, and speaking to women's groups. You can find her on her blog, as well as on Twitter and Facebook.

Maretha Retief

Maretha is a child of Daddy God, a wife to a loving husband and mommy of three blessings from God. Having been born with a disability she writes with a purpose to bring the hope of Christ in spite of circumstances. You can visit her online at SeasonsWithChrist.com.

Sheila Rhodes

Sheila Schweiger-Rhodes is an author, speaker, blogger and the founder of "JesusGlitter." Jesus Glitter is about looking for Jesus in the everyday moments of life. Each week you can find inspiration at JesusGlitter.com where Sheila encourages others to "Be the Sparkle!" She is the author of the soon to be released book, *Holy Unrest: Where Conflict Meets Your Calling.*

Sheila has been described as <u>deeply</u> passionate, profoundly uplifting and completely authentic. She loves anything that sparkles! Her passion is to share the message of God's redeeming love and offer hope to those who have been wounded by life.

Dr. Karen Michelle Ricci

Dr. Karen Michelle "Shelly" Ricci is down to earth but Kingdom-minded. Her desire is to speak to the heart of the reader, regardless of age. Her background as a Traditional Naturopath and Biblical Wellness Counselor (along with her life experiences) have given her a unique ability to write about deep topics, in a light-hearted way. She has a passion to see the body of Christ healed and restored. She currently lives in Dallas, TX with her husband and daughter. Together, they write music, lead worship, love to travel and try out new recipes. You can join Shelly on Facebook in her Naturopathic healing group, Shalom Total Wellness.

Phyllis Sather

Phyllis is an ordinary woman serving an extraordinary God. She has been the joyful wife of her best friend Daniel for 33 years and became a stay-at-home mom 31 years ago after retiring from a management position. Her children have graduated now and are doing well. She is grateful for the years she's been able to do exactly what she always dreamed of doing. How many people can say that?

Phyllis blogs to encourage younger women at Write the Vision. She has published several books, including her favorite, *Purposeful Planning*.

Alana Terry

Alana is a pastor's wife, self-diagnosed chicken lady, and Christian suspense author. She and her family live in rural Alaska where the northern lights in the winter and midnight sun in the summer make hauling water, surviving the annual mosquito apocalypse, and cleaning goat stalls in negative forty degrees worth every second. Find out more about Alana or contact her at any time at AlanaTerry.com.

Jessica Wright

Jessica L. Wright is an author, speaker and certified Christian Life Coach through the American Association of Christian Counselors with over sixteen years of ministry experience, who desires her restored life usher in great hope to those battling with guilt and shame. Her passion is to see broken hearts restored to wholeness, teaching others their Identity in Christ and Freedom from the past.

Jessica's favorite place is with her love, DD. They have been married for fourteen years, have two beautiful children and live in Seymour, Texas. Her joys are being outside, spending time with the ones she loves, laughing and reading. Connect with Jessica at JessicaLWright.com.

Contact Information

We would love to hear from you! You can send comments, questions and prayer requests to the following address:

Heather Hart
P.O. Box 1277
Seymour, TX 76380

Or connect with us online!

Email: heather@candidlychristian.com
Twitter: @CandidGals
Instagram: CandidlyChristian
Facebook: CandidlyChristian

Made in the USA
Columbia, SC
12 September 2018